Snow

Snow

twice orphaned / once rescued

by

June Gale

PHOENIX PUBLISHING
Canaan, New Hampshire

The poem, "Gifts," on page 113, is reprinted with permission of Macmillan Publishing Co., Inc. from *Collected Poems* by Sara Teasdale. Copyright 1915 by Macmillan Publishing Co., Inc., renewed 1943 by Mamie T. Wheless.

Gale, June
    Snow: twice orphaned / once rescued.

    1. Holloway, Snow Meader.   2. Mental illness —
Biography.   I. Title.
RC464.H585G34   362.2'092'4 [B]   80-21941
ISBN 0-914016-74-1

Printed in the United States of America
by Courier Printing Company
Binding by New Hampshire Bindery
Design by A.L. Morris

Contents

Preface

SNOW'S STORY will reveal different truths to different readers. To a psychiatric social worker, it discloses strands of causation in the development of a severely paranoid personality. As the details fall into place and the pattern is revealed, it becomes clear that Snow's childhood marked out a road he would feel compelled to follow. This will be uncovered in Part 1.

In Part 2 he tells the details himself. Grown, but restless with unsatisfied longings, he married, and married again, looking for wives who would be to him all the things his mother never lived to be. They could not: Snow became resentful of them and suspicious of virtually everybody who crossed his path. Frustration and rage ensued; his emotional outbursts, as well as his adamant withdrawal into the husk of himself, reflect an unrecognized determination to destroy himself. He failed to accomplish this. It has been one of his few failures.

Part 3 will explain how the social worker tries to uncover and resolve this inevitable tangle.

This book is offered to all who are interested in others' inner journeys and their findings. It follows a single thread, though the work of discovery obliges our hands to unwind several spindles for the causes of aberration and trauma are knots left woven into the fabric.

We who call ourselves healthy and would diagnose and prescribe for others' pain first must acknowledge that we can see only a little way into the cruxes of their lives. It is impossible to declare a suffering human being "psychotic" or "neurotic" without knowing, for example, the accretion of fears that raced through his infancy, childhood, adolescence, maturity, marriage, and on through confused thickets of failure or error or helplessness.

Part 1

Background

1

The Pregnant Child

CORA CLARA shook her head and sighed her disgust at her mother's incessant questioning. The way she tossed back her black curls spoke her defiance as much as the pouting expression on her face. "I *told* you," Cora Clara said, visibly attempting to control her temper, "Suzie is comin' by for me. We're all changin' to slippers after the game for the *dance*. The Grange is tenderin' a little tribute to our team. That's why the bag, Ma. I explained all this *before*. I'm not excited, Ma, just surprised you don't believe me. It's always the same. You're after me for every breath I draw—every step I take," she said, and sighed again as she moved toward the front door. "Well, I'm goin' now. Suzie's outside waiting." She took up her bag. Her mittened hand opened the door and slammed it behind her.

It was a cold November night even for Boothbay Harbor. There was someone waiting in that cold for Cora Clara, but it wasn't Suzie. Charlie McKenney was there, his borrowed sleigh tied to a tree at the foot of the hill. He didn't think to take the bag from her, he just took her hand and half dragged her down the road. Stumbling with panic, the child—for she had seen but sixteen summers, all in this Maine coast town—now trod a downward path so often faced before and since by pretty, passionate girls with no preparation for youth other than the blind, overbearing discipline of their bigoted, stubborn parents. Tonight, for Cora Clara Meader, the destination was Bruns-

Cora Clara's home on Bay Street, from which she ran away to elope with Charlie McKenney.

wick, the decision powered by fear.

Charlie McKenney lived with his family across the Androscoggin River in Topsham. It was a milltown, crowded now with immigrants from Ireland and Canada who rushed to fill the need for cheap labor. Crowded tenements hung over the river, which served both as a source of power for the mills and as a conduit for the town's sewerage. The year was 1902, when the grandees in Boston demanded yards and yards of cotton goods for their clothes and homes. River towns in New Hampshire and Maine were sucking in cheap labor and squeezing out profits through souls and bodies. In 1880 three McKenney brothers had brought families with them to Maine. One settled in Topsham; one across the river in Brunswick, the third northwest in Lisbon Falls. Living was primitive and schooling limited to the few hours not spent in the mills.

For Charlie McKenney and Cora Clara Meader a tawdry little marriage ceremony was performed the following morning in Topsham. The night had been spent on endless miles of snow, in endless hours of hopelessness. The Congregational minister and his wife did their best to give the rite an air of benediction, but they had seen too many such dreary starts, too many similar attempts to cover a childish moment of abandon with a heavy blanket of adult responsibilities. They could see this moment of reckless abandon only as a curtain raiser to the heavier burdens of cruel work, ill health, and debt.

Angelia Hallowell Meader, Cora Clara's mother and wife of Alonzo, a respected seafaring captain of Boothbay Harbor, faced the closed door after her only daughter had snapped the thread that had bound her. Angelia was rigid. She could not make herself turn away from the door. The present slipped out of her usual control, and suddenly she, too, was sixteen again. Dreadful, scorching humiliation crowded out her anger as she lost herself within her past.

Her mother had been strict—New England strict—but that hadn't stopped Snow Baker from slipping onto their back porch all through that August when his boat had been on the ways. It had been simple to glide down the stairs in bare feet to meet his ardor and his promises. She, too, had given promises, and finally had given him herself. Their plans were simple. When Snow made port again, he and Angelia would be married in the village church, as proper as you please, with white veil and Sunday suit and all the neighbors there smiling and wishing the best for the handsome couple. She would sew and make ready until January came again. Then the marriage would fittingly be followed by a boat trip to Portland. When sailing time came again, she would return home to join her mother as another waiting wife.

The burning humiliation spread until Angelia felt dizzy and drew herself back, momentarily, to the present. At last she turned away from the door and toward a chair, powerfully aware of her solitude. Alonzo was five years in the grave, and the three boys—Snow, Frank, and Orrin—had followed their own paths. Frank was eagerly approaching the time for his examination as a master mariner, young Orrin was already fascinated by the ocean, by its smells, and its risks, and was destined to follow the waves all his short life. Only Snow failed to show the expected enthusiasm for the life at sea.

Alonzo had sailed with Angelia's father, Captain Hallowell, on his three-skysail-yarder, a Down-Easter built in Bath. Although ten years younger than the captain, Alonzo nevertheless spent his shore days in friendship with Angelia's father. Believing himself independent of need, Alonzo had never seriously considered marriage. There were no tasks for a woman in his life, as there was no realization of any incompleteness within himself.

Angelia's betrothal to Snow Baker had never been made known. She sobbed in her mother's lap, not when the news came that Snow had been washed overboard, but when life moved within her and she felt helpless to solve this mystery alone. As usual, Alonzo was with the family. Almost as he would have performed any favor for his captain, he married Angelia at the parson's house, setting sail that same day on a slow voyage, loaded with lumber, toward southern ports.

Angelia had not allowed herself a long cry. The busy hours had pushed hard one upon another without restraint from her. Her father attended to the securing of groom, minister, and sleigh. Her mother pressed the starched petticoats and the ruching, and she took over the lamenting herself. Angelia had nothing to do but obey the orders that guided her through each passing day and sleep each night away in dreamless exhaustion. Alonzo had touched her hand in marriage and was gone. Snow Baker was so buried within her that it was as though it were he who had torn himself away from her for a second time, and indeed Angelia was left at home to await the birth of his child. It remained like that all her life.

The *Seamaiden* tied up at East Boothbay early in July, and most of the families concerned drove over to meet their menfolk. Angelia never thought of going. She had little Snow "Baker" to take care of, and Alonzo's present return seemed to her really no different from his others. He carried his duffle to her room before cleaning up for supper, but she hardly seemed to care and fitted herself into her ready-made position without any conscious feeling of reality. The baby's crib was near her bed, and her preoccupation with little Snow had caused her to fuse Alonzo with the baby's real father until, for her, one became the other. With a peculiar twist she had, however, withdrawn all emotion from a husband to pour it onto her baby, Snow. She stiffened in pride—in her manner and language—and remained strict, unbending, and domineering throughout an emotional life. She looked forward to the time when grandchildren would come under her influence, as she knew that would be her one chance to reopen her buried joys.

Snow

In a quick succession of years Frank and Orrin were born between voyages, yet Snow continued to be treated with the overindulgence generally reserved for an only child. Orrin was already ten years old when Angelia became pregnant for the last time. She hadn't wanted any of these later children—Alonzo's children—and had formed the easy habit of letting the boys play along the waterfront while she hastened through the household chores, then withdrew to rock and knit. The Hallowell homestead was hers now, alone at the top of the hill, backed by mast-high fir trees with the harbor in front, houses and docks spread around a great crescent. It was 1886, a time when Boothbay Harbor was a busy fishing port with sardine factories spreading out across the harbor from the older village. Alonzo was now a successful man in his own right, a master mariner with a small fleet of Down-Easters, two-and four-masted schooners built in Maine and sailed by good Maine men, and carrying lumber, lime, ice, and granite. They returned with cargo needed locally.

In 1887, curly, black-haired Cora Clara joined her three brothers in the house on the hill. Snow was twelve years old now, a tall boy full of ambition and selfishness. The tender, warmhearted affection Angelia had showered on Snow, but withheld from her other sons, she poured forth again on Cora Clara. The tiny girl had the high cheekbones of her mother, although she would never grow to Angelia's pinelike height and strength. She was the sweet adored sapling that bent with the prevailing wind and smiled in concurrence with the passing mood—a perfect foil for a determined mother.

Frank was already in active charge of Captain Meader's fleet when his father, now an old man, died quietly at home. Angelia took the body back to Wells, Maine, and watched Alonzo lowered into the ground alongside his mother's grave. Frank moved his family to Massachusetts and opened a shipyard and repair shop in Fairhaven. The mother-son ties between Frank and Angelia had never been strong, and now the break was made cleanly and totally. Angelia had inherited her share from the Hallowells and retained the Boothbay Harbor property. A sizable estate left by Alonzo came to her as well, administered by Judge Kenniston, who was to remain a wise and respected friend and advisor.

Orrin had never attained the physique of his brothers, yet he yearned for the rough life at sea. He signed on any southbound ship that would have him. On one such trip he contracted yellow fever and died, alone ashore, untended. They had called him Orrie, but his

Fore-and-aft rigged Down-Easter, of the type in Capt. Alonzo Meader's fleet, close hauled in Lobster Cove.

Snow

spirit was at home only on the sea, and he had broken maternal ties
almost as soon as they were formed.

> *Orrie get your dory*
> *There's a herring in the bay—*
> *Orrie got his dory*
> *But the herring got away.*
>
> Anonymous

At the time of Alonzo's death, Snow was living in Waltham, Massachusetts. He had been to high school in Boothbay and spent a year in Augusta studying engineering. There he stayed with Hallowell cousins, living among city comforts and culture. He discovered his interests leaned toward watchmaking, so he set out for Waltham, the primary center of fine watch production.

Before leaving Augusta, Snow married Carry Lord, the affable daughter of the local Congregational church minister. He had courted her in the parsonage, and the whole affair was conducted strictly and correctly. Angelia went alone to the wedding to bid this Snow farewell. She wore black bombazine trimmed with velvet and carried a woven metal bag. She remained handsome and unapproachable. She had ruled at home, but now all three sons and a husband were beyond her reach. Only Cora Clara remained.

Angelia maintained her house, kept a fast horse with buggy and sleigh, and put up a winter's supply of vegetables each year from her garden. She continued knitting black stockings of fine cotton yarn for Cora and herself, as she had done for all her children. Feeling the need for a wood chopper, a fire builder, and a talkative adult companion, she rented rooms, one at a time, to retired sea captains who had been Alonzo's associates. Her only indulgence was to sit alone in the unlighted front room, rocking and watching the sea and the stars.

Now Angelia sat in the hall chair, her heart somewhat softened by her reliving of the past. She knew there had been no Suzie outside. Cora Clara was gone now, just as Snow Baker and Alonzo and the three boys had gone before her. The flow of memories had helped.

The Pregnant Child

She was feeling the cold of this November night. Her chair was far from the kitchen, the warm heart of the house. She folded her arms around her and made her way back.

Silas Warner, her current boarder, had pulled a chair toward the open oven door. He was asleep, so Angelia did the dishes and noisily set about putting them away. She fixed the house for the night and tugged at Silas until he was awake enough to hear her reminder to bank the fire before he went to bed. Satisfied, she went to bed herself, the litany of those who had gone from her slowly running through her mind: Snow Baker, Alonzo, Snow, Frank, Orrin—all were beyond her reach. And now the last, Cora Clara, was gone, too. All that remained was the prospect of grandchildren.

2

Birthmate

WEEKS PASSED without any news from Cora Clara before a letter arrived. After their marriage and a short stay with Charlie's family in Brunswick, near the mills, Cora Clara and Charlie were living in their own house across the river in Topsham. Both had secured jobs in the mill, and although Cora admitted to a daily tiredness come nightfall, she assured her mother that they were making out fairly well.

Wasting no time, Angelia packed a bag and went down to visit her daughter. She found the house, a quaint white cottage, one and a half stories high, and covered with vines and boasting a small yard. She immediately set about establishing her role as the dominating force there. During the long days she scoured floors, straightened drawers and closets, and prepared the meals. She acted as if Charlie was not there at all, and it was difficult for the young man to hide his embarrassment. She continually offered unsolicited criticism of his plans and dreams and berated him for not providing enough income on his own to keep Cora out of the mills. She showed displeasure and scorn for all his words and actions, and she seldom even allowed him to be included in a direct conversation.

She remained in Topsham a week. She did up the curtains and purchased little comforts for her daughter, who now displayed quite clearly the fatigue of an overworked expectant mother. Finally she returned to her own home, but not before letting it be known that she

The house on the Androscoggin River in Topsham, Maine, where Snow was born.

would be back to stay for the month before Cora's due date. She also made sure to let Charlie know that she thought her daughter was much too pale, that it was undoubtedly his fault, and that he was surely a terribly selfish young man to put such a burden on a young girl.

So it came about that the grandmother-to-be moved to Topsham in March 1903 and sat out the cold and wind watching her daughter approach her day of delivery. Together they sewed and prepared. Angelia never showed any affection toward her unforgiven child, but she ran the house perfectly and everything was in readiness on April 15, the day Charlie was sent to fetch the doctor. Cora Clara was quite frail and followed suggestions without fuss. She was small and the baby large; labor extended into the next day, the sixteenth. After the doctor delivered the large head, he administered chloroform to Cora

Clara in order to repair the torn tissues. Cora suffered slight hemor-
rhaging and lay half unconcious until late that second night.

As Cora lost consciousness, Angelia had swept the baby, a healthy
boy, into her arms and taken him to the warmer kitchen. Cooing
softly, she bathed and bound the infant in band and shirt. Laying him
softly in his small basket, she said aloud, "Sleep in peace, my little
Snow."

Charlie also sat in the kitchen, watching his son's unfocused eyes
open and shut. Kept out of his own bedroom during the difficult
delivery, Charlie had had only a glimpse of his wife. Just as her life
had nearly been lost to him in his absence, so too now were lost the
mysteries and confidences of early parenthood. As he watched his son
closely, his mind repeating over and over, My baby . . . our baby . . .
my son. But Angelia had taken over as if the child were rightfully hers,
as if Charlie's thoughts were childish nonsense. And little "Snow"
she had called him. What had happened to the name he and Cora had
decided on? He was so confused and uncertain while Angelia seemed
so confident and knowledgeable. It wasn't right, but his son was quiet
and comfortable, and he did not let himself think of it any further than
that.

Cora Clara remained in delicate condition and did not sit up until
her son was a week old. By early May she was spending a good part of
her days by the sunny south window, but she didn't venture outside
to the garden until June. Her boy was sturdy, with his mother's curly
black hair, and eyes that were slowly changing to hazel. The molding
of his head showed wide cheekbones and a broad forehead. Already it
seemed evident that, above anyone else, little Snow would reflect the
physical appearance of his grandmother Meader.

Angelia returned to Boothbay Harbor to do her belated spring
cleaning. She put all her power into it. Gardens were planted late in
Maine, so hers was in as soon as her neighbors'. Her last boarder had
left for The Sailor's Refuge, marking the end of Alonzo's surviving
friends, so William H. Call, a Grand Army man, moved in and remained for many years. Things at the house in Boothbay Harbor
continued with little change. There was no horse in the stable now,
but Mr. Call did errands on foot. Alonzo and the children were all
gone, but Cora Clara was not very far away, and most important, now
there was her grandchild—her little Snow.

The summer passed with only the scantest news reaching her by letter from Topsham. In September, Angelia decided that the only way to know for sure what was happening there was to return and see for herself. She sent word ahead that she was coming into Brunswick by train and again set off to visit her daughter and grandson. In the past she had always made her own way by carriage from the train station to Topsham, but this time Charlie met her in Brunswick.

"We've moved," Charlie said in response to the question she had asked only with the expression on her face. "We decided to leave the cottage and find something closer to the mills. I'll take you right there—it's not far." He looked thinner and almost lifeless; his face was devoid of any discernible expression.

Indeed, their new home was not far from the train, so they set off on foot. Charlie led Angelia across the freight tracks and up a cinder way toward the back of a tenement. Angelia stared a moment in silence at the broken step, knowing but not wanting to believe that up this rickety stair and over this decrepit porch she would find an equally squalid apartment—the new home of Cora Clara and her little Snow. Charlie held the door open, and she pushed past him into the sitting room. There, half upright on the sofa, was Cora Clara, a thin pale wisp of a girl with ivory skin and wavy black hair. Angelia's eyes darted about searching for the baby. She sighed in relief at the sharp contrast her little Snow presented to his mother's sickly pallor. His eyes were bright, his cheeks rosy; and even strapped in as he was, his body seemed a bundle of healthy activity. He held his full-barreled body erect in the small cart and, displaying neither shyness nor recognition, calmly accepted the attentions of this strange woman who loosened his buckle and swung him to her shoulder. "My little Snow," she cooed, "my little Snow."

Again Snow became grandmother's baby boy. She supervised his whole day and tended his every need. As before, the household immediately came under Angelia's control. She cleaned and scrubbed and polished; she caught up on the large pile of wash that had accumulated in a back closet; she saw the potential in the apartment's large, sunny rooms and soon had them all neat, attractive, and convenient. Money was tight, and Cora Clara was three months along again. She had been feeling badly from the beginning and had quit work the previous month. She had not been eating well and suffered from continual tiredness and weakness. Charlie had turned to his uncles for help, but they had large families and times were bad for them too, with many men out of work. When Cora Clara was carrying

Snow

her first baby, she hadn't seen a doctor until the later months, but this time the doctor had already been called twice. He prescribed a better diet and as much exposure to the sun as possible.

Angelia took over her daughter's care, preparing balanced meals and getting her outdoors when the sun shone. She never missed an opportunity to remind Charlie of his shortcomings and all the burdens he had selfishly placed on her daughter's shoulders. Despite her mother's efforts, Cora Clara never regained her full strength. Early in 1904 her second child, to be named Orrin, was delivered stillborn. Cora remained bedridden, her suffering increased by her sorrow, while Angelia continued to run the household. Again Charlie was lost in a flood of indecipherable emotions, so he gladly allowed his mother-in-law to control his wife, his son, and his home; he concentrated on minimizing Angelia's opportunities to remind him of his responsibilities for Cora's condition and the death of their child. Thus life continued in the apartment. Charlie went to the mill each morning, his thoughts and emotions locked behind dull, lifeless eyes; Cora Clara slowly regained her strength, her thoughts and feelings, too, well buried; and little Snow growing each day under the watchful eye and close supervision of his grandmother.

By early summer of 1904 Cora Clara had rallied and was up and about enough to convince Angelia it was time to return to Boothbay. She packed her bag again, content for the moment to be leaving behind a well-ordered household, full pantry shelves, and an active, healthy grandson. She wanted to take her Snow along as far as the station, so Charlie went with her. "Her boy" could say a lot of words now and ran about on sturdy legs. "Gar take Gar boy," he kept saying as they prepared to leave the tenement. His perpetual smile and good nature showed the world a trusting child not easily upset by what happened about him. As she mounted the train steps, he did reach out his arms and begged, "Gar take Gar boy!"

Birthmate

3

The Abduction

BILL CALL had taken good care of himself and the homestead, and Angelia could pick things up about where she had left them, as if she'd been gone for days rather than months. Perhaps now she sat more often in the darkened room, but as always there were those long black stockings to knit.

Judge Kenniston had done well with her holdings. Real estate was going up, and they had foreseen the new summer visitor trade well in advance. Angelia owned a number of investment properties, which she now shrewdly renovated so they would be ready for the higher short-term, seasonal rentals that could be charged. A house could sit unused all winter and still command more rent in three months than had once been collected from twelve months of use. Artists started showing up in Boothbay Harbor with their watercolors and oils, intent on producing a summer's worth of sketches and paintings. Old fishhouses were rented out, but one group of artists soon developed a central dining room idea. This spread and others built cabins among the pines out on the high, jutting promontory behind the Meader house. A new art colony developed there, called Mount Pisgah, and Angelia became a reliable dining room manager. Her cooking skills made her famous in the area. As the colony grew and roads and walls were built, vines planted, and paths cut through the woods, Angelia became an important factor in the busy three-month season. She had always dressed becomingly in good clothes, but now she made dec-

Dining hall of the art colony on Mount Pisgah.

orative cotton dresses that showed off her straight back and beautiful head. Her hair was gray by now, yet her face remained as smooth and creamy as alabaster.

After the busy summer season in Boothbay she spent most of the winter each year in Brunswick. On each arrival she immediately took over, as though she knew the family had been eagerly waiting for its head to return. Charlie looked thin and stooped, his hacking cough almost incessant now, but he kept doggedly working at his mill job, leaving home with a kiss each morning and returning promptly at the same time each evening. Snow would run down to the corner to meet him and always received a good ride back on a gentle arm.

In October 1906 Cora Clara gave birth to her second living child. It was a girl, with facial features much like her father's—but named, of course, Angelia. Cora Clara again was sickly and remained in bed.

The Abduction

This time she was destined never again to take up a full life. The doctor decided she had tuberculosis, and apparently the disease was well advanced. He suggested she be bundled up and kept on the open porch as much as possible. So, as Snow advanced from infancy to boyhood, he developed a single vision of his mother: a sweet, pale lady with black curls, always waiting on that narrow porch; soft voiced and always heavily clothed; wrapped during the winter months in a borrowed fur coat.

Angelia stiffened at the doctor's diagnosis. Her lingering dislike of Charlie hardened into a solid mass of hatred. He had stolen her daughter and had become the cause of her death. She did nothing to hide her hatred, throwing her accusations at him whenever possible and treating him with open scorn. Whatever effect this added tension had on Cora Clara was masked by her advancing disease. She was far too weak and resigned to reveal her reactions.

When Snow was eight years old his mother died. The fact was kept from him at the time—it wasn't until years later that he was able to connect the events of that day with the truth; and it was years after that before he knew the name of the illness that had taken his mother. Yet he was keenly aware of the change that took place in his life that day. It began the way most days began, with breakfast, a morning of intense play, a hearty lunch, and another afternoon in the backyard. A bright sun was melting the ice and snow, making streams and puddles where he formed the mud into makeshift dams. Intent on his play, he didn't notice his grandmother standing on the back porch, but when she called to him he obediently brushed the mud off his hands and followed as she walked across toward the neighbors. Angelie was with Grammy, but she was too young to tell him what was happening and Grammy offered no clues. They made their way next door, to the great house with many rooms, fully furnished. It was an old farmhouse, once the homestead for a farm that had included the present sites of most of the surrounding tenements. There was a long ell at the back of the house stretching out along their street, but the front entrance was on the thoroughfare around the corner.

On this afternoon Grammy led the way in through the side door and left them in the kitchen. He and Angelie stood waiting in the room absorbing the different sights and smells while Grammy's excited voice drifted through the hallway beyond the closed door. "Try to keep them quiet," he heard her saying. "I'll come for them after five, but in the meantime don't let anyone talk to them. Don't let anyone know they're with you. If you have to, hide them." He couldn't make out any more, and in a few minutes Grammy came back into the kitchen, this time with the lady who lived in the house. Without further words Grammy hurried back, using the side door.

Snow and Angelie played a while with some toy blocks and looked at a picture book, but they were both confused and restless. The lady treated them kindly, giving them milk and fresh-baked cookies, but she seemed disturbed and uneasy. Snow knew something unusual was going to happen to them, but he trusted Grammy to make it come out right. Darkness came, but still Grammy did not reappear. The lady tried to amuse them, but there was something about today that made it different from the other times they had come to visit her.

At last Grammy came back, carrying an overnight bag in one hand and clutching their coats and hats in the other. Something strange was definitely happening to them, and real fear clutched at Snow. Grammy herded them into the darkened living room and shoved them under the piano. "Don't make a single sound," she said, emphasizing each word. It was cold in the room. He and Angelie both shivered, from fright as much as from the cold.

After what seemed like hours the kind lady came into the room and told them they could return to the kitchen. She gave them cereal and prunes, but tonight the Force tasted dry, the prunes sour. Snow was wondering whether this little game was finally coming to an end, when suddenly they were being rushed about again. The lady helped them into their coats, and suddenly they were out on the street, walking away from their home. After several blocks they turned up a walkway leading to a big house. "This is where the Bowdoin College librarian lives," the lady said, as if she expected the words to have some meaning to them. "These people are going to take care of you for a while, until your grandmother picks you up."

For three days they roamed freely through this large entrancing house. They were not allowed to go outdoors, but the newness and lushness of the house so awed Snow that he hardly gave the outside a thought. He couldn't imagine what might be going on in his home and never worried about his family. He just knew Grammy would in some way dissolve all troubles and bring him comfort and happiness, although he couldn't be that certain about his sister.

Finally Grammy did come, carrying their belongings and announcing that they were going with her back to Boothbay Harbor, "for a visit." First it was the train, then the boat trip; the new sights and people blocked out his questions and homesickness. He arrived in the harbor for the first time and was settled into the upstairs front room. It was his very own room. He felt at home, running in and out to Grammy just as he had always done anywhere they'd been together.

4

Snow at Boothbay Harbor

I T WAS Bill Call who created the earliest morning sounds. Snow had waked in the night, but exhaustion kept him from wondering what was to happen next. He had slept to wake refreshed and ready for a day's activities. Wood chopping had been going on in the back shed, but the thuds against the sides of the woodbox in the kitchen below him brought him upright in bed. He slid into his clothes quickly but stopped short of the rumpled shirt he had traveled in the day before. The door to the upper hall stood open, and he eased himself downstairs and into the kitchen. Angelie, who had slept with Grammy, was already at the table waiting to start her first breakfast. Grammy saw he had no shirt, so she stepped to her ground-floor room to get a colored blouse from the bags they had brought with them.

These households, overlooking a great Maine harbor, were not like those found inland along the Atlantic coast. The region had no real farm atmosphere, no hilly pastures approached through narrow stone-walled lanes. The plots of land of the seaside homesteads were carefully laid out with fruit trees and summer gardens; porches had been added to some in recognition of warm evenings and the restfulness of sitting comfortably in the open. A hammock and some high-backed rocking chairs sufficed. Before bedtime children sat on railings and steps. Sometimes a little boy would be rocked to sleep by the rhythmic squeak of a rocker on a loose board or by the slight crunching sound of the metal ring swinging from a hook that held the hammock safely off the floor of the piazza.

That first summer was one of investigation and trial and error. It was a long trip to Atlantic Avenue, but Snow had the courage to walk down the hill to the north rim of the harbor. He'd scurry back when he was alone. Mr. Call made him a little red cart, the first in a series made with Bill Call. Later he would build them alone. Friends called the children Angelie and Snowie, and they passed the summer clothed in the attention and sympathy that neighbors lend to children who have suddenly been orphaned.

So the new life began. The strong cord holding grandmother and grandson was felt more and more by each. Snow had visual promise of an ever devoted "mother," while Angelia Meader had her arms around the shoulders of her beloved Snow, her only love. Sister Angelie was still very young. She had her brother with her, and the home with her grandmother seemed much like the one she had left. Elderly Mr. Call lived in the home, and it was he who took charge of the two children that first summer while Angelia was working at the Art Colony by the day.

Young Snow felt a sense of growing responsibility, and this summer seemed to him his first grown-up year. Before school opened he would walk to the harborside alone to watch the fishing and cargo boats unload. Sometimes he would drag his little sister along, but she kept tumbling to her knees and slowed his trip. At the end of the day they would both make their way to the top of the hill, up the winding, pine-arched lanes to the door of the great dining hall. Here they would be joined by their grandmother, who would have in her hands some goodies left from the dinner. With bundles in her right hand and Snow's hand in her left, with the trudging baby clutching Snow's other hand, they found their way back down through the sweet-smelling evergreens, down through the dark tunnels toward home.

The day after Labor Day, 1911, was Snow's first day at his new school. He could attend the third grade in the tall white schoolhouse at the foot of his street. Angelie was entering kindergarten, so they joined their neighboring friends as they formed an increasing line of noisy, teasing children on its way over the brow of the hill to the schoolhouse.

Snow's spick-and-span appearance and his sparkling brown eyes won the approval of teachers from the start. He had plenty of attention and thus learned quickly. His grandmother had the same multiplication table cards she used with her children, so it was her practice to

Snow

drill these two grandchildren as she had her own. The cards were well worn. As quickly as they were needed Snow had each table at his finger tips: 11X12 was as sure a possession as his 1X2. Through those early grades Snow was always selected to recite before the class when a school board member visited. His teachers could count on his memory, and his beguiling delivery made a most favorable impression for the teacher. Later it was he who spoke lines on parents' day before the whole school, and he who won on declamation day. His report card spelled the pride of a doting grandmother. Angelie could never seem to equal these achievements.

Pennies were the key to life and pleasure. A penny bought a large pickle and a hard tack at Leon Trask's small glass-fronted store. This store was on the way from home to the secondary school; there was a full-fronted flight of five steps from sidewalk to its well-worn door. It smelled good. A great array of necessaries was grouped inside. To the right was an area containing such sundries as pins and needles, ticking and batting, black hose and heavy wool socks, rubber boots and oilskin slickers, small wares for personal and household use. To the left were packaged foodstuffs, and across the width at the back the living, moving business of the day took place. The huge jar of dill sat here jammed with giant faded cucumbers, the top layer floating up-ended in the liquid. Next was a row of hinged boxes containing crackers or cookies available for any hand to weigh out a pound on the open scale. The last customer in each succeeding box would find many broken dusty pieces in his pound. The counter surmounted bins for peas and beans, dried prunes and apricots, and all manner of dried foods to be cooked all night and all day on the black range at home. A wall cupboard contained Castoria, Epsom salts, bicarbonate of soda, Scott's Emulsion, and other patent medical preparations for the alimentary tract. In the adjoining shed, barrels of kerosene were stored. There, gallon cans were refilled and spouts sealed with a small potato.

The penny was generally carried in a clenched fist or tied well in a handkerchief until it was placed noisily on the counter near the pickle jar. A courageous child might keep the owner quite busy fishing for a particular pickle, elusive but large. The accompanying crackers were in an open barrel close by. A fellow could pick his own. Licorice, horse whips, Gibralatars, peppermint sticks, horehound, cinnamon bark, all-day suckers, and many more—Snow carried his candy away in

Snow at Boothbay Harbor

red-striped paper bags. Often a hungry boy would make a meal with what his hard-earned pennies would fetch. Ten pennies were made in a single hour posing for artists in the art colony—those were handsome penny earners.

Snow was stunned one day on returning from school to hear the abrupt and threatening voice of his usually contained grandmother. It was the close of the first marking period in school. "Never, never shall I hear that name again. You are Meaders now, you are my children. Sign your papers Meader." It was further explained to the two children that Gar had adopted them for sure.

At age ten Snow took a summer job as stableboy at Charlie Sherman's Livery. He worked twelve hours a day cleaning stalls, brushing horses, soaping harnesses, going over the carriages with a feather duster. His earnings: 25 cents a week and a baked bean supper on Saturday night. Saturdays he worked later. As he grew taller, he could harness the horses and bring them up the ramp to the main floor where he took directions as to which surrey or buggy was to be hitched. In a year's time he was driving fares all over town, meeting boats, handling luggage, depositing summer people as far away as Newagen and Southport. When only a fifth grader in school he was driving couples up the long pull to the town hall in Boothbay where Saturday dances were held. He would wait in his surrey within earshot of the scratchy music and good-hearted laughter. He could see many courting couples strolling about or leaning from the windows of the spacious hall. At eleven-thirty the young people poured down the steps and scattered to their vehicles. Then began the race down that long, straight dirt road for the return to the harbor. That baked bean supper at the Sherman's and the tip from his passengers made the 25 cents a week seem acceptable compensation. Work early became a religion, service his goal, and any appreciation his reward for living right. Snow was satisfied.

The seasons appeared and passed in quick succession. Boothbay Harbor was somewhat isolated from the outside world, even if that world was only the state of Maine. Many families had inbred and there were often found the retarded, the insane, the recluse, the old-fashioned spinster type, the resentful and suspicious types.

When going home from school, Snow early learned that it was wise to wait at the foot of his hill and there to join the other children returning from school, since old Frank Reed, who lived alone, would hide behind his hedge close to the roadway to make queer noises as the children passed. If a child was alone, he squeezed through the shrubs and made a thrust toward the child, grabbing at skirts or trousers. Snow hated this; he felt great physical disgust and loathing. He'd run for dear life to escape such clawing hands. Wyman Bennet lived over the wall from the Meader house. He had two children, a boy and a girl. One day the group of children were playing together when, by accident, a stone Snow threw hit a Bennet child. The boy ran screaming into his father. Mr. Bennet stepped out of his house shouting fury and revenge. No attempt was made to verify the story or discover the intent of the players, no calling on the grandmother for mutual decisions—just an insatiable temper driving him to catch the culprit and measure out the whipping he felt any stone thrower should have, especially when the victim was his child. Snow made a circle through the woods, darting behind trees in his search for safe cover from this fiend. His only thought was to reach home, where he knew he would be defended from anyone or anything. But he lost his breath, slipping on the pine needles as he made his turns, and he was caught by the distraught father. He was thrown to the ground and cuffed about the face and ears by the enraged man until he was numb and the man exhausted. Snow waited a few minutes before he tried to rise and make his way back. He could hear nothing; his head ached and his vision was blurred. It was a vicious beating indeed. Snow's one thought had been that if Gar knew about it she would give Mr. Bennet what he deserved, a good whipping. He had that much faith in his grandmother's defense of all his actions. She was a dear and wonderful being to him. Actually, Snow stayed outside long enough to recover his equilibrium so that when he went in to supper he would not need to mention the chastisement.

Mr. Call was old. He could not hurt anyone. He was mellow and happy, and he made everyone in the late Captain Meader's home feel secure and tranquil. He had patience with the children, especially with young Snow. He showed the boy how to use tools and how to make and mend toys and keep his cart in use. It was important that a boy have a cart in Boothbay Harbor. Wood was burned in stoves in winter, so in other seasons much time was spent gathering fallen logs and boughs in the pine woods. Snow pulled his cart up the long hill

Snow at Boothbay Harbor

Interior of Luther Maddock's sardine factory.

beyond the art colony, where he would make a load of wood, tying it well to his cart. In late fall the wood had to be hand-sawed and stacked neatly in the back shed. Mr. Call taught him to keep his tools in top shape and put them away in their proper places after use. The old gentleman was a wise teacher of good habits that stayed with Snow all his life. This important cart had other uses. It hauled the little sister when her feet wearied after a long excursion to the harbor or beach. It brought back food from the local store. It had other exciting uses—it earned a precious, often rare penny for its owner.

Mr. Call had spent some time at Luther Maddock's sardine factory, working on the lower level where men were employed handling the fish on their way through the steaming rooms. This opened the path for the children to pick out fresh, unrelated fish they could collect and

Snow

sell from door to door. This was a needed free service for the factory and a great opportunity for the youngsters.

The coast of Maine was sprinkled with canneries from Eastport to Portland. The Meaders' town had two busy and productive concerns. As a loaded boat nudged into its wharf the factory whistle would notify its workers that they should show up to earn their money. Women with thick aprons over long cotton dresses and men in tall rubber boots would converge like ants tumbling from a disturbed hill. Once alongside, the large buckets of unloading fish with ocean water were hoisted by derrick and swung to the flat top of the two-story building. A rope was yanked, tipping each load into a slightly slanted sluiceway that ran as does a slow-moving brook, bearing sardine and other odd fish toward the conveyors where the women prepared the fish for the canning. They spread them out on mesh trays and passed them on to the men's floor below where the heated ovens partly cooked them. Later they were returned by dumbwaiter to the women standing at long benches, packing the tiny fish into the cans head to tail. They worked so fast one could barely see their hands moving. As they ran out of fish they'd call, "More fish!" The foreman, who pushed the racked flakes back and forth, would stop and empty a tray at a given space. The tin tops were then emplaced after fish oil and flavorings were added. The cans were conveyed to the soldering room where men sealed them and placed them in sterilizers. Later they were inspected and spot-soldered when necessary, then cooled, wrapped and labeled.

The children who turned up were really doing a great free service. They climbed the ladder to the roof, carrying their pails. As the mixed fish landed in the wet troughs they quickly picked out the sunfish, the smelt, and other small fish caught in the sardine nets at sea. The more alert and coordinated the small hand, the bigger the haul. Snow could fill his buckets in no time, descend the ladder, and start his route through the Art Colony. The cart, with its portable slatted body, held his pails while he hawked from door to door selling a dozen smelts for 10 cents. Before Angelie was old enough to recognize coins, Snow used to give her "Those great big nickels while I'm satisfied with these little dimes." The day came when baby sister became aware of this con game and went crying to grandma for restitution.

Angelie had collected enough coins to change into a 50-cent piece. She and Snowie had decided to cross the inner harbor footbridge and find something she would like to buy in the busier shopping area. She hadn't gone far when she tripped and dropped the precious silver

Snow at Boothbay Harbor

The first inner-harbor wooden footbridge where Angelie lost her silver piece.

piece. It rolled for a few seconds, then slipped between the boards and sank in the deep water. She created quite a hysterical scene —crying, demanding, blaming, and exhibiting much pain and stress. She couldn't understand how she could have lost her money.

An older couple soon caught up to them and stopped to inquire what tragedy had overtaken the little girl. They were quick with sympathy and dried the tears with the gift of a replacement. They left two consoled children and continued across the inlet. Snow tucked the coin in his pocket, and taking Angelie's hand, walked along. Soon he spied another summer couple coming toward them. He quick-wittedly coached his sister to repeat the act. "Cry again, Angelie. Cry good and loud and we'll see what happens!" Her little face was still red and damp from the previous occasion, so she only had to repeat a few words and look down through the flooring. This couple was completely taken in and made restitution to the obviously stricken, tiny native child.

Snow

Snow and a group of boys used to meet and spend time on the wharves. If a fishing boat lay alongside and was unloading, the men would throw aside unwanted species. The boys would gather these and take a meal home. If a coaler had been unloaded, they'd fill up pails by picking up stray pieces along that wharf. It became apparent that small pieces could fall through the worn holes in the planking; at low tide they could be retrieved from around the pilings under the pier on the muddy shoreline. A boy wouldn't lose a chance to kick a few extra toward these holes. Snow sold a pailful for a nickel up along Bay Street and Mount Pisgah. He always pulled that red cart of his on these profitable sallies.

Capt. Alonzo Meader had left a comfortable home, well cared for and well furnished for that period. The last Down-Easter in his fleet had been named *The Cora Clara* and was the end of that era. Judge Kenniston had been a wise financial advisor and a real friend, and Angelia was a careful woman, and she had the strength of a man. She could swing a hod of coal or carry an armful of wood like a man. Each stick was set in the kitchen woodbox as though there were a dozen more to follow. The household was run strictly on schedule. Bedtime was held to, teeth were brushed, and clothes were hung in place. Church was attended, truth was upheld, and children did not interrupt their betters. However, Angelia was frugal. Nothing was wasted, and no article that could be mended was to be replaced; every article that might have a need was to be saved. Bits of string rolled up, paper smoothed and stashed in a cupboard, nails straightened, scraps of cotton left from dressmaking were converted to aprons. "Waste not, want not" was for her a serious matter.

The white house on Bay Street had a kitchen ell, an attached woodshed at the back with a small barn beyond. There were perhaps five acres, enough land for a small orchard, grapevines on the walls, a vegetable garden, and flowers toward the street. Angelia liked flowers and cultivated them with ardor. Mr. Call cut the grass and produced the vegetables. He would bring them washed to the back door. He and Snow would cut up the firewood and stack it before the first winter storm. A large pantry was filled with fruit and vegetables put up in Mason jars. Under the eaves dried apples hung, and winter squash, carrots, potatoes, and other roots were stored for winter. There was seldom butter in the house—this would have been a luxury—but good black molasses was not overlooked for an annual spring tonic,

Snow at Boothbay Harbor

"for the blood." For cooking, fat saved from chickens sufficed. Crocks held corned beef and glassed eggs. Fish came from local supply; salt, spices, and other staples, from Trask's store.

There was a privy between the shed and barn and a pitcher pump at the kitchen sink. The house had well-trimmed lampwicks, with sparkling glass chimneys— a colorful shade for the living room. A shelf held iron and brass candlesticks that were carried to the bedrooms. The handling of wood matches was a serious lesson early taught and overseen. Lanterns had hooks in the woodshed and barn; also in the outhouse. They were returned to the shed when not in use.

Livery stables supplied transportation to inland rail centers, and boats plied between the many island homes, as well as connecting Portland, Bath, and Boothbay Harbor. In fact, all dry goods, hardware, all drug supplies and repair parts, and produce packed in iced crates from Boston markets arrived by boat. The landing was the center of town at docking time. The youngsters were there to see and smell, grown-ups were there to pick up goods; sometimes ten surreys with horses and drivers were lined up to drive passengers to Spruce Point, Southport, or Edgecomb. Small boys, including Snowie, knew when bicycles were expected by the local hardware store, and they hung over the rail to see who could spot them first. The older boys lined up with dollies to run the cargo off. When the tide was out the boys ran the empty dollies rattling down the gangplank, but leaned forward with long strides pushing their loads up to deposit them at the edge of the wharf, then down again on the run to keep their places in line. Sometimes a rope, strung between a pair, added help to the load going up. But it was the smell of the harbor waters, the oil from the engines, and the air from the pungent holds that made his memory cling to these busy arrivals. Sounds, too, counted, the clanking chains that lifted or lowered the gangplanks according to the tide, the laughs, the shouts, the orders given in rough salty language; but all these followed the toots from the whistle giving warning long before the boat was in sight.

Little Snow from Topsham could hear the first toot from each incoming boat. He flew down his hill, across the new footbridge that later spanned the inner harbor, to be at the wharf's rail before the bell to reverse engines was sounded in the engine room and before the bow hawser was thrown on shore. Add four more years, and this old young man of twelve years would be hired out as driver to the plushiest livery stable in town and sit upright in a surrey, with high-stepping mare, waiting for the lady, the traveling salesman, or a family to ascend and tell him, "To the Bay House," "To Spruce Point," or simply, "Home."

Occasionally, Angelia took her children to Portland, Augusta, or nearby Bath. Trips were made by boat and were for business purposes, but soon enough they returned to their structured, closely supervised life in Boothbay Harbor.

> *Adrift! A little boat adrift!*
> *And night is coming down!*
> *Will no one guide a little boat*
> *Unto the nearest town?*

from "Time and Eternity"
Emily Dickinson

Snow at Boothbay Harbor

5

Last Will and Testament

IT WAS HERE in this isolated community, setting its own mores, that Snow became aware that giggly little girls with starched petticoats had something they were halfheartedly trying to hide. There had been no father image to follow, as from birth he had depended on Grammy, his sister, and the teachers whose darling he was. He was a sturdy fellow, but time found him playing with the girls. He had begun to show distrust of men; only his devotion to, and appreciation of, old Bill Call was to remain throughout life his true faith. He loved elderly men and could never do enough for them. He lived up to the ideals of these mature men, who had achieved a proper way of life. Not unexpectedly, he took a deep dislike to his uncles, Snow and Frank. They represented fathers too weak to keep track of their own children. All his life Snow was never to buy any stock in his contemporary man.

Snow was thirteen when he became aware that his grandmother was not well. She bustled about the house in an increasingly frantic way. Things were done, but the mainstream of organized thinking seemed to have reached its delta. Bill Call was gone; Snow was the man around the place. He had not thought of the possibility that dear Grammy might leave him, too. Winter was beginning to soften when March winds were becoming noticeable. There was no commotion among the neighbors, no unusual number of visitors, no calls from the family doctor, but Snow was upset when Grammy peeled the

potatoes and dropped the skins into the pan of cold water and the
edible parts into the waste. Then a day came when Grammy took the
children into her room to point out some treasures in the worn,
swelled-top trunk. The three went down to its level on their knees. A
key was produced and the contents revealed.

The trunk was lined with cotton print. The top tray had two lids,
the smaller one at the left covered a good hiding place for papers and
old letters. Snow was shown a will made out on Judge Kenniston's
stationery complete with a red waxen seal. Dear Grammy read it aloud
to the two children in front of that musty-smelling trunk. The first part
worried Snowie; he felt a queer wave go over him with the mention of
"last will and testament" and "being of sound mind and body." He
realized suddenly that a premonition was becoming fact. Grammy
was really not sound of mind all the time, and she sat rocking an
increasing number of hours a day. He knew what a will was, but
"testament" sounded like the Bible. This was like a solemn church
service. Grammy was pointing out that his uncle Snow was to receive
five dollars, since he held two positions and owned his own house.
Uncle Frank was to receive five dollars, for he also had a steady income
from his tugboat company in New Bedford and his shipyard in Fair
Haven. But to her daughter's children she left her home, her worldly
goods, and all her investments including their income. Lawyer
Plummer's name appeared somewhere and was to be recalled later.
She then closed and locked the trunk and told the children where to
find the key if it were ever needed.

Each day after school Snow found Grammy sort of stranded when
he reached home. The fire needed replenishing; the tea kettle was
empty; these were little things that he could quickly do so domestic
life could start rolling along again. Some mornings Snowie would get
Angelie's breakfast and take coffee in to his grandmother; some days
he had to find her clothes for her. Often he'd notice that supper was
ready but Grammy did not eat. Finally, one day in March dear
Grammy could no longer get out of bed. She asked for tea; she had
Angelie fetch a shawl but she assured the two children she'd be all
right in a minute. Still these two lonely youngsters did not call in the
neighbors. They really did not know what was about to happen.
Grammy wanted Snow close to her. He held her up while she sipped
from a spoon. Her throat was dry and she was very weak. Suddenly
she appeared to faint. Angelie was frightened and begged Snowie to
run for the doctor. He thought he'd better, too, so he rushed out into

Last Will and Testament

The S.S. "Westport" on which Aunt Carry and Uncle Snow came to Boothbay Harbor.

the bleak weather and started to run across lots, by the high school, down over a bank, around the end of the cove, and along Atlantic Avenue to the doctor's house. Breathlessly Snow gave his message and received the assurance that the good doctor would be there as soon as possible. Snow returned home the way he had come, except that it was all uphill this time—the road to run, the bank to scramble, the woods to fly through, the last backyard to cross. Scarcely had Snow reached the bedroom when the doctor's horse pulled up outside.

Somehow things were arranged. A neighbor lady spent that first dreadful night with these stricken children. Uncle Snow and Aunt Carry in Waltham had been notified, and they would arrive by the next day's boat. Cold struck Snowie; he hated this uncle. He had been afraid of him, even mistrusted him when his family made a yearly visit. Life was going to be difficult, he knew.

Snow

Uncle Snow was a large, impressive man. He was head of a household of women. In his overbearance he had reduced his wife to a housekeeper under strict rules for care and orderliness. His older daughter, Margery, was eleven, pretty but flighty. Isobel was seven and already trying to gain a recognized place in the family. Their father dominated all phases of their lives. Meals were formal and eaten in the dining room. Clothes were spotless and conservative in style. Promptness was imposed. Rubbers had their places and were used when indicated. School and church filled every Sunday morning. He was a parish committeeman and a deacon for the First Congregational church. Outwardly his life was without reproach; inwardly he was a cruel hypocrite. During the usual business hours he was a department superintendent at the Waltham Watch Factory. Evenings and weekends he held office hours in his home as an optometrist. He liked to be thought of as a doctor.

It was this uncle who pushed open the door of his mother's house on Bay Street and began giving orders. The children shrank from him. Aunt Carry tried to embrace them but gave up and left the scene to her husband—and a harsh scene it turned out to be. "I have decided that you children shall return with us," he said. "We can make the room. You can attend school with Margery and Isobel. Now tell me, where did your grandmother keep her things? Do you know if she had any papers?"

Angelie didn't answer, but clung to her brother. Snow felt sure of himself when he answered, "Everything is settled; we're to stay here." Uncle Snow tightened his grip on the situation but could get nowhere. "You're fond of your aunt Carry. I'll let her talk to you." Aunt Carry worked on him, and finally, seeing his efforts were useless, Snow gave in completely. Aunt Carry pried out all the information needed and even bribed the children to make the trip to Waltham.

So it was that the children collected their treasures together, including Snow's bicycle and his blue serge knicker suit. The suit represented to him both manliness and Sunday occasions. Into the trouser pockets he had stuffed a drawstring bag containing all the loose coins that Grammy kept in the kitchen cupboard. Snowie insisted that he be allowed to keep what he thought should be his spending money. But after a hurried consultation with his uncle and a tussle with the boy, his aunt removed the suit from his luggage and

Last Will and Testament

took it into another room. The next time Snowie saw his precious clothes he was in Waltham but its pockets were empty.

He was an obedient boy, but sullenness was building up inside him. He tried to like his two girl cousins who would share their house with him, but they treated him like an outsider and never made him feel at home. Angelie fared better; she was younger and a girl, and she seemed to fit in with the all-girl group. On her first morning she sat on the railing of the front porch. A neighbor passing down the street stopped to ask who she was. "My name is Angelie and I come from down Maine. I live with my uncle. My brother's name is Snowie and he come from down Maine, too."

Snow was put into a small room on the third floor of his uncle's home on Fiske Avenue. The house was typical of the 1900s, a boxlike building two and a half stories high, with a covered piazza across the front and a small covered back entrance. The interior shone with many coats of varnish. All the woodwork throughout the rooms was coated with this varnish. The kitchen and the bathroom were half paneled with narrow matched deep ocher boards. All other walls were papered: there was a living room pattern, a dining room pattern, a hall pattern, and there were bedroom patterns. These were selected from the paperer's book left at the house in advance of any work that was planned. The hall papers were rough textured and dingy; the bedrooms' wallpapering had small flowers in raw colors; the living room paper had a bold pattern with awkward scenes. Snowie's small room was well furnished with odd pieces, all painted with the same dull white paint. His white iron bed, his two straight chairs, his four-drawer bureau, his one-drawer dressing table, and his woven-seated rocker all indicated a room obviously prepared for a girl, but at the time he only wondered what his Grammy would have thought about it.

On the very first night the Boothbay children arrived their uncle Frank came over from Melrose. His brother guided him immediately through the front hall to an upper chamber. The meeting was kept secret, as were the nearly monthly meetings during the following years. When they returned to the living room the conversation was stilted, and the expression on Aunt Carry's face one of worry and curiosity. She appeared to disapprove of their behavior, but she clearly wanted very much to know how the decisions would affect her and the girls. Snowie and Angelie didn't have to wait long to discover how they were to be treated. The orders started almost at once. With great sacrifice, Uncle Snow said, he had offered his home to these penniless children. They must work in the house to make it possible for him to keep them. Angelie would help with the kitchen work, setting the table and washing the dishes. This involved waiting on table and doing little errands for all members of the family, of course. Snowie would take out the rugs each week and beat them on the lawn. He would keep the cellar clean and fill the woodbox in the kitchen. Actually, during that first year he sawed and chopped two cords of wood his uncle had bought for the house. The pieces were packed one at a time by hand, into tall, even stacks against the cellar wall. Snowie could never play ball with the boys after school unless he could hurry through some tremendous job after four o'clock each schoolday. Saturdays were even worse. In effect, these children were used as poor relations to serve their patrons and spoil their cousins. The little girls caught onto this game quickly and abused the goodwill and silent patience of young Snow.

To prevent confusion, his uncle had begun on that first day to refer to Grammy's Snowie as "Snowden," a name that became a monster for the boy. Aunt Carry was stiff and demanding, perhaps because she was frightened of what her husband would say on his return each day if the waifs had not done more than was expected of them. Windows were washed often, rooms swept, carpets shaken out. Punctuality was enforced and table manners were stiff and rigidly enforced. Not only did Snowie have to do outside drudgery all day long and to abide by tough rules at home, but excellent school work was also a must. Homework had to be done and marks had to be good. A report card with a low mark meant a beating on Fiske Avenue—at least for Snowie.

At school one day a spinster teacher came down the aisle sniffing as she progressed, with one long-nosed sniff to one side, then a matching sniff to the other. She came to Snow's desk and said, "Aha!" She pulled him from his seat by his ear, marched him to the front of the room, and sat him down. "You have been smoking."

"Not in school, ma'am," he said truthfully. Boys smoked Sweet Caporals at an early age in Maine. He was reported to the principal, Mr. Drake, and was sent home in disgrace. Uncle Snow had received the dread news. Before supper, without explanation, Snowie was forced to leave the house and go down the road to Mr. Drake's home. The uncle had a lighted, evil-smelling cigar clutched between his teeth. Before going up the steps to the front door, he carefully set this

Last Will and Testament

cigar at the edge of the step, keeping out of sight as much as possible. Then the bell was rung, and the nervous wait started. A half hour later, his ears ringing with warnings and his triumphant uncle walking behind him, Snowie left that house, noting that Uncle Snow took a step aside after the door shut behind them to retrieve his still smoldering and saliva-tipped cigar. That evening Snowden heard a series of threats and warnings of future punishments for repetitions of his sinful deed. He was terribly upset, but he vowed to himself that this pair of oversized men would never catch him this way again. He would be more careful hereafter.

During vacations Snowden was expected to earn money. His regular job was as busboy in the watch factory cafeteria. His uncle secured this job for him, but he did not leave it at that. He warned of the dangers of wasting his wages, and he inaugurated a weekly accounting session up in the little white room. A common desk key opened the drawer of the dressing table where Snowie kept his money. Shoveling walks in winter and cutting lawns in summer also added to his increasing store. His uncle counted the savings and noted the amount. If any had been spent, he wanted to know just where it had gone.

One week there was a sum of four dollars with no accounting. Uncle Snow waggled his long index finger and accused his nephew of spending too much for candy. Snowie unabashedly assured him that he had locked the drawer and had never been back again that week. His uncle, unable to bear either the lie or the boy, took a step back and struck a heavy blow across Snowden's face. There was no argument that time, but as the months slipped by and the situation was repeated, the punishment turned to a formal beating with a strap. Uncle Snow was large; Snowie was short but compact. Snowie talked this over with Angelie. They tried to figure out who it was who was taking the small amounts from that drawer. Not the uncle and aunt surely, but possibly Isobel or Margery? The children set about trying to catch the thief.

Uncle Snow became obsessed with this need to vent his spleen by punishing his nephew. He had no sons, and couldn't love the son of his only sister, now dead. The boy was too obedient, too polite, too patient. Or perhaps too discerning? In late afternoon when Snowie came in through the back entrance, changing to slippers as he had been ordered, he would catch sight of his uncle's long finger seeming to ensnare him into the living room. There were no words wasted, just the two-flight trip up to that third-story room, the bend over the bed, and the walloping. The strap was heavy, and the hand that wielded it heavier still. Snowden would beg for a reason, any reason. His uncle would think up all kinds of small infractions as excuses.

It appeared that Margery spent more dimes at the corner store than the other children. She also had the same type of table in her room, one drawer, one common key. There came a day when this twelve-year-old younger cousin had a large sum of money which she took from here to there along the nearby group of stores. The storekeepers were amazed. Mr. Putnam felt that her father should be told. He knew that Mr. Meader was not in the habit of allowing any of the children to spend money without permission. He dropped in that afternoon and reported the matter to Mrs. Meader. She was quiet and unresponsive. However, she passed the story on to her husband as soon as she could get him into their upstairs bedroom alone. "Angelie, of course," he said. "Two of a kind, those bastards." Angelie was called up for an inquisition. She had never come in for any of this unnatural suspicion and hate before, as her brother had absorbed all of it. She cried, denied, and almost fainted. She remembered that all the children had been to Sunday supper with a lady down the street only a day or so before. The matter of the earlier stolen money had made her so nervous that she had spent the whole hour on a stool near the knees of this loving friend. No one could ever accuse her, she felt. It turned out to have been a wise move for such a young lady. A sum of money was taken from a pocketbook left with the coats in a bedroom. Angelie was marched down to Putnam's store to face the owner.

"Oh, no, Mr. Meader, this is not the girl who spent so much money here. It was your own daughter, Margery." Uncle Snow pushed his niece ahead of him, through the door and down the street. They visited three other places, but the answer was always the same. Later, Angelie asked the dear lady to speak for her to prove to her uncle that Angelie had had no opportunity to go through the pocketbooks during the party.

Once more Snowden was to see that finger beckoning him upstairs and hear the hateful sound of his new name. This time the accusation was so farfetched and the humor so black that the boy feared for his own safety. He stood his uncle off. Stretching for the white rocking chair, he dared the older man to lay a hand on him. The strap was ready, the arm raised, but they were struck down by the wild swing of Snow's new-found daring. The chair hit the uncle, surprised him, cowed him, and sent him from the room incredulous. That was the last of those one-sided attacks.

Snow and Angelie held a family consultation. It was more urgent perhaps than that, because Snowie would be sixteen the next day and he had reached a final decision. He could not live in that household another day. He could now legally leave school and procure a work permit. He'd find a room and support himself. Angelie begged to leave, too, but he insisted that it was out of the question. Snow would take what money he had saved over the months, although it was short by the amount that Margery had taken. He never received recompense for the stolen sum, an apology, or any other sign of recognition.

Snow left the Fiske Avenue house as soon as it was dark. Angelie would put his clothes together, make a bundle of them, and drop them out her window as the clock stood at midnight, that same night. These children were thirteen and sixteen years of age. They sought no advice of outsiders. They had been forsaken by those who had procreated them, by a grandmother who had seemed perennial, by blood relatives who rejected them even while offering them shelter. Angelie was afraid to remain alone, but it could be arranged no other way, at least for the time being. Her brother tried to calm her by saying they could keep in touch through friends they had made in Waltham. Then he was gone.

6

The "Santino"

S NOW KNEW he could have his job at the cafeteria full-time. There was a need for more help, and he already had worked there part-time. His uncle had recently switched jobs and was now working for the E. Howard Watch Factory on Felton Street, so Snow set about finding himself a furnished room. The Waltham Watch Company had extended its building half the length of Crescent Street along the Charles River. Snow knew that whole area well, so he walked to Adams Street and found a room a block or so from Crescent Street. In company with a boy he knew, he strolled over to Moody Street for a bowl of soup. Moody Street was the shopping area in Waltham. It ran from the Newton line, sloping toward the Charles River, crossing it, then making a slight rise before forming a great T with Main Street, which ran east and west. City hall, the common, banks, and a few office buildings faced Main Street. Fiske Avenue met Main Street near Banks Square called the "Head of Main Street." There was another way of reaching the factory from this West End, using back roads and the Prospect Street Bridge to come out at the north end of the building. Snow felt confident he could carry on his new life without the worry of regular or chance meetings with his uncle. He knew they would not be likely to meet going to and from work or at any local store. As it turned out, Snow worked from April to July, when the two-week vacation period closed the factory, without meeting his uncle once.

42   During the first few weeks, after the initial arrival of the two Maine children at Fiske Avenue, they had often walked over to Putnam's Store in the West End. His was a small neighborhood store that carried a variety of items for emergencies as well as everyday life. It was open longer and more days of the week than the regular downtown stores. It was here that Snow had met Fred Munster. Fred was the milkman who brought the day's supply from the H. L. Stone Dairy. He hefted in the round quart bottles in their iced-off wooden cases. Large and friendly, Fred knew everyone in that district and spotted the new children immediately. "Where're you children from?" he had asked.

"We come from down Maine," Snow had answered.

"Well, you don't need to tell me. You sound just like my cousins in Boothbay Harbor!"

The long friendship had started right there. Fred's cousins were Richard and Mabel Lewis, who had lived diagonally across from Captain Meader's house. They had been two of the group involved in the experiences of Bay Street and only recently separated from Snow and Angelie. Fred asked them to ride his horse-drawn wagon to Watertown and back, and they accepted unhesitatingly. Fred was married and his youngest child was twelve years old. For Snow, this man immediately represented a father, someone he needed, someone to trust. The milk business fascinated him, at least that part represented by a fine horse and special wagon. Snow had driven fast horses in Boothbay, but the idea of a daily trip with deliveries made to thirsty children in need of health-giving milk appealed to him immensely. He found great romance and satisfaction in Fred Munster's job. He worked at night, with 8:00 A.M. finding him at the end of his run.

Now, out on his own, Snow sought Fred again, finding him, as expected, at Stone's Dairy. Thus a new habit of life began for Snow. He would catch a few hours sleep after his stint at the cafeteria, then make his way quickly across the Prospect Street Bridge and onto upper Main Street in time to swing aboard Fred's wagon. He spent many nights making the rounds, learning how the tally was kept and how the route was followed. On free days he visited the plant to observe all he could of the dairy's operation.

Snow now made use of this friendship. When the vacation period was forced on Snow, he turned to Fred, hoping he might be able to get him a job at the dairy. Fred was sympathetic to Snow's plight, but there was nothing he could do. "I'm sorry, son," he said, "but you're

Snow

still too young. Company policy, you know. You just hang on for another year, and when we get an opening I'll see that you get the job."

Snow was disappointed but understood Fred's position. He turned his attention toward finding another job, at least to get him through the vacation period. But before he had an opportunity to do any serious looking, his uncle Frank from Melrose showed up with a ready-made job for him. Frank still owned that shipyard in Fairhaven and needed extra help to see that a sailing vessel was repaired and sent off to sea again by a contracted date. His son, Junior, the same age as Snow, was scheduled to spend the rest of the year living and working on the five-masted schooner *Santino*, and Frank wanted Snow to join him. The boys would be paid wages, and the ship's cook would take charge of them.

The *Santino* was an old schooner that had been a workhorse up and down the east and west coasts of the two American continents before the construction of the Panama Canal. After a lull in her need, during the second decade of the century, she had been put into heavy use again for the duration of World War I. Now her owner, reading the signs of the decline in demand for her use, had sold her to a South American trader. The new owner in turn had placed her in the Meader shipyard for extensive repairs. Thus, Snow's search for employment ended quickly.

Snow packed his bag and rode down to Fairhaven with Uncle Frank. He was introduced to some of his new coworkers, then given a short tour and history of the *Santino*. "Over a million and a half board feet of pine and spruce went into this ship," Uncle Frank said, "and two hundred tons of iron." Snow could see that this was going to be more work for a blacksmith than the carpentry or sailmaking he had first envisioned. Wire rigging set up by turnbuckles was used in place of hemp. Steam winches handled cargo, sails, and anchors. Electricity furnished light. There were steam heat, telephone connections, the latest windlass, steering gear, pumps, and sounding equipment—all very different from what he had expected.

For the first few weeks he and Junior lived onshore in a room up over the office at the yard. But as the ship was readied they moved into the captain's quarters, eating meals like those in a boardinghouse ashore, and sleeping in airy staterooms. There were eight white men in charge; fifty Portuguese Negroes were employed.

Work began in earnest. Snow was assigned to the boss blacksmith. With a fourteen-pound hammer he would strike the spot on the

The Santino

heated iron indicated by the smithy. A rhythm was achieved that kept the two hammers apart: using a small peen hammer, the blacksmith tapped the hot iron where he wanted the blow struck. As he withdrew his arm, Snow, having swung the sledgehammer over his shoulder, would come down on that spot with accuracy and weight. To halt the action, the boss dropped his peen lightly on the anvil. The piece to be mauled would be brought from the site and explained to the blacksmith. He would then heat the piece in the forge, holding it with tongs. After mentally planning his course, he would start the cycles with a tap. Snow would swing and hit. The tap would be repeated, and in perfect timing Snow would strike again. The iron would be turned this way and that until the repaired part was ready for use. The sledgehammer seemed to travel in identical orbits, the very weight of it carrying it back over the shoulder. The slight ringing of the peen on the anvil was a grateful signal to lower the great hammer for a rest. Snow did this type of work all year. His arms grew powerful; his chest expanded to a conspicuous size; his hands developed into huge mitts. His timing and eyesight became one machine of extraordinary accuracy.

The two boys stayed at work until Saturday noon, then they were free to take the trolley to New Bedford to see a movie. They generally ate dinner in some small place and returned early for a long sleep. They got up when they wanted on Sunday morning and spent the balance of that day just loafing. On weekday afternoons they were allowed to stroll up the road to Fairhaven for a sundae or two but were rigorously watched over by Uncle Frank or the Negro cook. There were no experiences with girls, either in an informal way or during stolen night hours. The year Snow reached nineteen was to be filled with a rush of emotional waves much as depressions in the sand are the first to be flooded by an incoming tide.

The *Santino* was ready to put to sea the following May, and the boys teased Uncle Frank to be allowed to sail with her. The romance of the ship and the sea was built into their blood by this time. They dreamed of sailing out through Buzzards Bay to the Atlantic, on down the coast to warmer climes, but Uncle Frank would not even consider it. The boys begged and beseeched, but the uncle was adamant. The *Santino* set sail without them early in the summer, passed the Florida peninsula, and was never sighted again. She and all those aboard her were lost—or so Uncle Frank reported. The official listing of wrecks has her sinking during a storm on her third trip toward the Indian Ocean. Those who sailed her were indeed lost.

Snow

Part 2

Snow's Recollections

7

The First Marriage

WITH THE completion of my job on the *Santino*, I returned to my room on Adams Street. I had to find another job, so that first morning back I set out on foot for Stone's Dairy, over by Waltham Highlands Station on the West Side of town. I took the Prospect Street Bridge route, avoiding Fiske Avenue and any possible meeting with my uncle Snow.

Stone's was actually a processing plant, not a full-operations dairy. No cows there, but plenty of horses—twelve of them—and a carriage house full of freshly painted red and black wagons. The drivers loaded them from the back, made deliveries from the side, and drove standing up. One lantern swung from the rear axle while another hung inside by the door. Metal-reinforced wood cases held a dozen quart bottles of milk or twenty-four half-pint jars of cream. There wasn't much in the way of pasteurization or refrigeration laws in those days. A smart buyer chose a milk source with proven high standards. From my friendship with Fred Munster I already knew Stone's milk was properly handled, chilled, and stored.

I knew, too, the whole setup and normal procedures for this dairy. There were inside boys who arranged each driver's load in stacks every few yards along the outside platform. As 2:00 A.M. drew near and the drivers began arriving, they would back into their slots and swing their loads onto their rigs, checking the count as they loaded. Each driver was responsible for every bottle assigned to his route. His tally book had to account for all the milk delivered or returned to the plant.

At nineteen, I felt ready to take on the world. I'd already supported myself for three years, had a good work record, and knew how to handle my money. As I'd hoped, Fred Munster had found the desired opening for me, and I was quickly taken on as a route driver. I'd handled horses before in Boothbay Harbor, so it was no trick to start out through the sprawling cities of Waltham and Watertown. A route foreman was supposed to take the trip with me for two weeks—or until each street, each turn, each house was known and visited quickly and in order. I set my mind to making a mental map, noting unusual features at intersections, driveway entrances, and the back doors themselves. After only one week I was allowed to go out on my route alone, without the foreman. I'd read the scribbled notes left by housekeepers and make all the necessary changes on each customer's page in my tally book.

In my own mind I saw myself providing a necessary service. Often, after climbing three flights of dark back stairs, I'd find a note asking me to leave two quarts instead of the usual one, but it never occurred to me that there was any reason to complain about the extra trip up and down those stairs for the 12 cents more it meant. Maybe I'd let out an occasional low whistle, but I never really let it bother me. I'd just do my job, hurrying from step to step, down long black alleys, across backyards, on and off back porches. I tried to be careful and not make any noise that might wake up my customers.

After a few months my horse, Ned, knew the route as well as I did. I'd fill my carrier with enough milk to cover two or three apartment houses, then wind my way from yard to yard, hopping hedges and dodging clotheslines while my trusty steed made his own way to the next regular stop. Of course, there were rarely any other vehicles on the road at that hour. My horse would start up as soon as my foot hit the step, and while I was checking the tally the wagon would move farther along the route, Ned in full command.

Finally we'd make our last delivery and head for the all-night cafe where all the drivers in that area met for coffee and doughnuts. I'd leave my wagon out front with the others, hanging a bag of oats over Ned's head. Later, it was back up Main Street and on through the early morning light. Quite often I'd hang up the reins and nap while Ned guided us home. Other times I'd take the reins and steer us along Boston Post Road to a little restaurant on Banks Square. After a while we were stopping there most every morning right around eight. The day people would be there, crowding in for a quick breakfast before

Snow

heading on to work. The food was good, and the people were friendly without being nosey. It was a comfortable spot; a good place to relax and eat before going home. I soon knew the faces of most of the regulars, just as they quickly began to recognize me and include me in their audience for jokes and stories.

There was one regular in particular who drew my attention. She was a pretty young woman, with squint lines of doubt around her eyes, who would come in each morning, brush back her dark, curly hair as she approached the counter, then order her coffee in a voice that was half demand, half plea. A little eavesdropping and a casual question or two got me her name, Evelyn Corliss, but little else. I continued to watch her quietly each morning as she drank her coffee, then hurried out to catch the trolley.

One morning the restaurant door swung open violently, and Evelyn burst almost breathlessly into the dining room. "Has the trolley come and gone?" she demanded of the whole room. The waitress told her it had. "What'll I do?" she asked. "I'll be late and I just know they'll drop me."

She seemed totally helpless and I reacted without thinking. "I guess I could drive you down," I said. "If you want."

She'd seen me there a lot, and I guess what with my clean shirt and overalls and my patent leather visored cap she thought I looked respectable enough. "Well, come along, then," she said, "or I shan't make it."

We climbed into my wagon and started talking as I directed Ned through the streets. Evelyn worked at Woolworth's, over on Moody Street. She said she'd been there since high school. And while she didn't seem too enthusiastic about her work there, she wasn't very optimistic about moving on to anything better. She apparently had no plans for living; no special interests and very little ambition. She accepted the attention I showed her enthusiastically. She struck me as someone who wanted to be spoiled, and I felt drawn to her right away. I turned the conversation away from her future, and we were soon chatting easily about nothing. She talked about her grandfather, a Gloucester merchant, and his house, which overlooked the harbor and where she had spent a good part of her childhood. Our similar backgrounds of seaports and shore life seemed to give us a common language. While neither of us could come up with any real interesting stories to tell, at least we were at ease talking to each other.

We reached Woolworth's too quickly and our conversation was cut

The First Marriage

short, but we easily picked up the small talk again the next morning at the restaurant. Soon we were meeting and talking every morning, and it wasn't long before I was outside Woolworth's every evening at five-thirty, waiting for Evelyn to get off work. I'd walk her home, where her parents would often invite me to stay for supper. In a very short time I was accepted almost as a member of the family. They switched dairies and started taking their milk from me, so I had the opportunity each morning to tiptoe under Evelyn's window while leaving the bottles. This intimate duty excited me, and I soon decided I had to have this pretty little girl in my arms.

Perhaps it was as much the Corlisses' family life as Evelyn herself, but I was drawn so strongly to that small family circle that I accepted any hint to spend my evenings there. My desires were fanned by the little notes Evelyn would leave each night in the neck of one of the empty bottles. "Had a great time last night," she'd write. "See you tonight." Or "That was fun last night. Don't forget, you belong to me." And "Must see you tonight, can't wait." I took to extending my free time so I could be with Mrs. Corliss while Evelyn was at work. I all but became her other child. The fact is that within a few months I was her son-in-law. I moved my few belongings from Adams Street to Evelyn's upstairs bedroom, with the household barely seeming to notice any change. Evelyn's parents continued to direct her life; only now we had doubled their responsibilities.

I all but smothered myself as I clung to my child-wife. We lay long hours together, my legs usually entwined about her as though to chain her to me. We had no adult plans to make, as Evelyn's parents ran our lives and we willingly deferred to them. Still in our teens, we were fulfilling our sexual needs without having to go through any maturing process. Evelyn was comfortable and freely allowed Mrs. Corliss to dominate her. I was content simply to find myself once again a pampered son.

This "let's play house" situation did not last long. Too soon, it seemed, we discovered Evelyn was pregnant. When she was eight months along, she and her mother went back to Gloucester to be with her grandparents and nearer the old family doctor. I stayed on in Waltham, working my route seven days a week. I slipped back into my old habits of sleeping in two shifts, eating wherever I happened to be, and doing my nightly run on the milk wagon. The whole situation seemed to make my marriage a minor, only half-believable fact. After the birth of our daughter, Cora Clara, I was able to get down to

Snow

Gloucester on a Sunday afternoon to see her. I found myself a distant fifth in importance there. The baby, Evelyn, and Mr. and Mrs. Corliss were all bunched together, with lonely Snow bringing up the rear. Once again I was on the outside.

Almost from the beginning there had been a lot of speculation by Evelyn's parents about what inheritance might be due me from my Grammy. Evelyn's grandfather in Gloucester was a member of the Boston Stock Exchange. The story of the missing will and the suspicious handling of my grandmother's property fascinated him. He made it his business to track down the facts. His lawyer in Boston, Sylvester Wayland, was consulted. Mr. Wayland agreed to look into the apparent theft. I rode into Boston to tell my story, and Mr. Wayland followed that up with two trips of his own to Boothbay Harbor—both in vain. He was unable to locate Mr. Plummer, who, as an associate lawyer in Judge Kenniston's office, had negotiated the original will. Wayland's investigation turned up only more questions left unanswered when Plummer disappeared. He had packed up and left the area shortly after Grammy died, leaving a faint trail that pointed toward California. Wayland also uncovered a similar story about the unsettled estate of an earlier generation in Grammy's family. The names of my uncles Frank and Snow turned up in that account as well. Two stories, so closely related, gave my version added credibility, and Wayland's conversation with Fred Munster's Boothbay relatives strengthened it even more. Fred's niece on Bay Street told what she knew of the Meader story. She said it was common knowledge in the neighborhood that Grammy was going to leave the bulk of her property to Annie (Angelie) and me. Wayland was impressed and decided to open a case against my two uncles.

With the initial arrangements concluded, I met with Evelyn, Annie, Mr. Corliss, and Mr. Wayland at Boston's North Station to catch a train to Bath. The station itself was an adventure for me. The smoky, cinder-filled air, the sooted, plush red seats and the choking, gaseous smoke that sucked through the car each time a door was opened filled me with an uncomfortable feeling of unreality. Things had certainly changed during the war. My last trip away from Boothbay had been made by boat and trolley. Now I was returning by train and automobile.

Annie was with us because she had as much at stake as I did. She

The Boothbay House where Snow, Annie, and the lawyers stayed during the court hearing.

had left Fiske Avenue when she was sixteen to become a ward of Evelyn's parents. Although she'd stayed with Uncle Snow three years longer than I had, Mr. Wayland felt money must be owed her as well. The last leg of our trip was spent in Mr. Corliss's Overland. Annie sat in the back seat with Evelyn and me, while Mr. Wayland rode up front with Mr. Corliss. We all put up at Harbor House to await our court appearance the next morning.

The following day I stood up in court and told the judge everything I knew about Grammy's will. I told him about her plans for our safety and comfort, about Uncle Snow's behavior all through the years we were with him, and about all the menial work that had been forced on me and particularly on little Annie. Filled with a sense of righteousness, I spoke right up.

"Uncle Snow and Aunt Carrie forced me to show them where Grammy kept her papers," I said. "They lied when they promised I

could have all my own things sent along to Waltham. Grammy left me 53
cash to use in case of an emergency, but that just disappeared without
words. And I did see Uncle Frank go upstairs with Uncle Snow to talk
privately that first night on Fiske Avenue. Annie and I were ignored
whenever we asked about our money for things we wanted. Uncle
Snow said we were lucky to have an aunt and uncle generous enough
to take us in and feed us. I know about that will. . . ." Here I almost
broke down with fury and sadness, but regained control and continued, ". . . about that will and about the home left to us in Maine and
about Grammy's plans for our future. She always loved my mother
more than her sons, and she loved me best of all. . . . I just know that.
She died suddenly and I didn't know enough then to run across the
street to get a neighbor or tell the story to anyone around there. Even
after they'd moved Grammy's body to the front room I went to her
trunk and pulled out all the papers in the top tray. I held Annie's hand
for courage, and we went to the front hall where there was an oil lamp
we could read by. I showed Annie every page and explained what it
meant. After the first lines Grammy had put in that her sons, having
good incomes of their own, should be given five dollars each. I never
really understood that, but now I see why she did it. The rest was to go
to her daughter's children. That's us. It was signed by her and Mr.
Plummer and had gold seals with a red ribbon at the bottom.

"Well, that helped us through the night and gave us something to
hold on to, since we believed we'd be staying right there in that
house. We put the will back in the trunk along with the other papers. I
was fourteen and felt sure I could run everything the way old Mr. Call
had taught me. Annie and I were still together when Mrs. Brewer
came and offered us breakfast. We could have told her about the will,
but as usual we just kept mum.

"Everyone tells me now I should have told the doctor or Judge
Kenniston or even old Mr. Trask, the storekeeper, but Annie and me
just waited together until our relatives arrived by the morning boat. I
had always been afraid of Uncle Snow. When he visited Grammy, I
used to feel sick to my stomach, and tried to stay out of his sight. There
was just something about him that I hated.

"I tell you, I saw that will . . . and other things, too."

I was finished, but my uncles were ready to respond. They told the
judge how they had sold the house and its contents, then divided the
assets three ways. It was decided that Snow and Carrie would house
Annie and me because they had the smaller family and more room.
From the first day on they'd kept detailed records, and these were now

The First Marriage

exhibited in court. They showed a charge of fifteen dollars a week board for each of us, as well as every item of clothing, each dose of castor oil, any carfares, all broken windows, toys, wear on the carpet, broken dishes—anything that could possibly be charged against us was written down in that book.

Well, things didn't go *entirely* against us. The judge lowered the room-and-board charges to a more reasonable rate of seven and a half dollars per week, which was still high for those days. But he had to allow all the listed items. Using our mother's third as a basis, Frank and Snow proved that Annie had used up all her share, but I still had twenty-five hundred dollars coming to me.

In his chambers the judge berated my uncles and their lawyers, calling them thieves and opportunists, but had to admit he could not hold them without Mr. Plummer's presence or some other corroborating evidence. Judge Kenniston was dead, and no other person alive could offer more than hearsay evidence. Mr. Plummer's unexplained disappearance was blamed on Snow and Frank, but no real proof was ever established. As for the earlier estate—most of Spruce Point—this property was unsettled, as it had been owned by Hallowells and never probated. Squatters had built cabins there, but the town eventually took it over and sold the land for back taxes. My uncles had been the executors of this aunt's estate, but her will had also mysteriously disappeared. However, in the end they never benefited from that shady deal.

I left the courtroom disappointed, my hatred of my uncles newly fired. The more I thought about it the more I realized how badly Annie and I had been used. Uncle Snow had taken us in simply to justify his and Frank's claim to the extra third of Grammy's estate (when the will actually entitled them to next to nothing). Then they'd charged us for every imaginable expense, from caps down to shoestrings, while leading us to believe we were working off our room and board with all the household chores we did. On top of all that, they had forced me to work outside jobs while forbidding me to spend even a cent of that personal fund. Shared blood or not, the very thought of those two uncles, from then on, brought a bitter taste to my mouth and a knot in my stomach.

Snow

8

The First Divorce

WE ALL RETURNED to the Corliss home, but soon I found myself longing to get out into the country again. I had a Model A Ford by then, so we often took Sunday drives over North Avenue in Weston. On one of those trips Mr. and Mrs. Corliss found a large, solid 1900 house in Acton that they liked. It faced the highway, and they were quickly dreaming up ways the whole family could make use of it. They would set up a roadside stand to sell duck sandwiches, tonic, and coffee; Mr. Corliss would make the trip each day to his job at the E. Howard Watch Company. Soon it became clear that they wanted the place. I was expected to buy it for them and change my occupation to one with set hours. Evelyn and the baby would remain with her mother.

"If you think that's all right," I said, in my usual way, "I'll do it." I found a job pumping gas at Smart's new fieldstone service station on Main Street in Waltham. The womenfolk had the house and stand, while I worked for one and all. Business didn't go well, so they pushed me into taking out a second mortgage on the Acton place. I came home tired each night, but for some reason my little wife no longer looked to me for those sweet, clinging, nightly comforts.

I began to notice other small changes in Evelyn. When discussions arose over the policies for the food stand, especially as to how to decide the financial priorities, she always took her mother's side. On late nights she always was sound asleep on my return from Waltham.

Often the baby was in my place on the bed, so I'd grab a few hours' sleep on the living room couch. I was clearly becoming an outsider in the Corliss family.

Two years of that was enough for me. I set about fixing up a small apartment on Winthrop Street, and when it was ready I gave my wife a choice: come with me to Winthrop Street or stay on with her mother. That burst the Corliss bubble all right. They were outraged, but there was little actual discussion and a settlement was quickly made. Only six hundred dollars remained after the sale of the Acton house, so this went to the Corliss family and I had my divorce. They bought another, smaller stand and camp nearer Walden Pond, and Mr. Corliss stayed with his factory job. They remained there some years, I was told.

Eventually I drifted to Wayland and found a position as chauffeur and groundskeeper at the old Terrace Gardens where Vaughn Monroe was making his reputation as a bandleader and muffled singer. I spent the days working on the lawns and parking area, then made a nightly trip in the truck to pick up meats and supplies from the stalls at Faneuil Hall Market in Boston. I never had any feelings about Terrace Gardens, its gaiety, the drinking, or the fights in the kitchens. Never jealous, I was content to be a handy, "I guess so" man. I was certainly ordered around, but I was kept running so much, just to get done what was required, that I never gave it much thought.

Sometimes the boss rode with me to Boston—he had affairs to attend to there—and I'd just push my way downtown to fight for a place in the market district. Occasionally I'd find a girl with whom I could spend some time. With no love involved, it seemed exciting and simple to get a girl, have her, and leave her. It didn't seem sordid or unfair; it just was. Eating around as I did, pulling up to a Waldorf or stopping in for coffee and doughnuts, I became friendly with a lot of waitresses. All that was needed was the question, "When do you get off today?" Norumbega Park, with its surrounding woodlands bordering the Charles River, was ten minutes from Moody Street. I had my car and my furnished room, and, after the social freedoms following World War I, girls were ready and willing. No one expected anything to come of these encounters.

As the years went along, I changed often from one job to another. There were girls who sought me out, but soon enough they'd move on to others. I didn't talk very much and never dreamed of settling down anywhere. My best friend, Fred, even though years older than I, had kept a girl outside his family. Somewhere in the back of my mind, this shocked me, but he was still my special friend. Fred's father had left

Snow

him a farm in Bucksport, Maine, so he moved his wife and grown daughter down East. On a visit later to that farm, I found a baby boy in the house. Fred's wife must have forgiven him. Our lives were separated for two decades—a black period for me. "Yes, ma'am," or "Yes, sir," seemed to keep me too occupied to look very far ahead. Every major mistake and each stupid mixup with people and the law seemed to result from my "Yes, I guess so"; "Why not?" and "I'll try it," answers. Work seemed the only way to solve anything, so I returned to the milk business, taking a route for Austin Andrews in Watertown.

Pretty soon I'd built my largest route to forty-five cases of milk. Families were satisfied with my promptness, and I kept Mr. Andrews happy by doing well on collections. This meant work after-hours on my own time, finding the bill payers at home on their paydays. I got smart at this, if I do say so myself. One man worked at night and slept by day. His wife would push an envelope under her door once a week. I never saw that customer, but I never lost a cent on that account either.

Money began to collect in my savings account. Many people left cash tips with their empties at Christmas. I came to a decision. It was time to raise milk for myself. I still dreamed of a life with a horse and some cows. First I hired a barn and pastured cows on land where today the Polaroid Land Camera is made. An old lady living near there often claimed one of my cows had wandered into her strawberry patch, and I'd give her ten dollars to pay for damages. She was really very poor, so even out of season I'd give her the money. Eventually I rounded up a few customers in Waltham and started a short route of my own.

Things were going too well. Andrews knew I was bringing him more money than any other driver, but he also learned about my private milk route around North Main Street district. He wanted it all. I was feeding and milking twelve cows, getting customers, and making deliveries—getting little sleep, but learned to take naps anytime I had a spare half hour.

Andrew's rigged up some scheme to bring me into his own business and sought a lawyer to draw up an agreement. We all sat around a table in a lawyer's office while they complimented me, offered a yearly bonus, shorter hours, security, friendship, and I can't remember what else.

"Come on, Snow," Andrews urged. "Sign this and we'll take care of you forever."

I just shook my head. "You can't mean all that's written here," I

The First Divorce

said. "I know you three boys well enough to pick up some trick in this. Let me think it over a few days."

It came to me later that the position they offered would be at a very low base rate of salary, and, after a couple of years, I might easily end up sweeping the dust from under their chairs. They'd have my customers, my cows—well, all of me. I refused to sign anything that time. No Andrews could be a father to me. I also had a strong distrust of the two sons, who were my own age. Not signing that agreement didn't stop me from entering into too many others later, but I never trusted anyone, and, somewhere deep down, past feelings of distrust and a fear of being used again began to sprout. The roots grew in a tangled mess; what came to the surface never bore true fruit or pretty flowers. The seasons of women, mistakes, and losses came out into sunlight and died within their cycles. But I could work, that was for sure, and I never failed to find something. Even during the deepest depression years of the 1930s, although it often meant accepting the most menial, underpaid positions, I was never without a day's pay.

Snow

9

The Second Marriage and Divorce

ABOUT 1935 I fell in with a French family—customers of mine. There were two daughters, and their old man invited me in for coffee anytime he could catch me. The younger girl had been ill, and I was subtly told she couldn't have children. I hadn't seen my own baby since she was two years old, and I didn't particularly like children. Old men I liked. There was something I could do to lessen their loneliness or poverty. Drunks on the street got sympathy from me. I'd sometimes take one home, hoping to help out, giving them an opportunity to do honest work. It never solved their problems, but I kept on trying. Women I didn't trust at all—I simply wouldn't believe a word they said.

The old Frenchman would keep me chatting in the kitchen until finally one day I noticed that Florie, the younger daughter, had taken some fancy to me. She had been divorced and her kids had gone to California with their father. Here she was at home again, with a maintenance job in a hospital, and on the make. I'd been through a low period myself. When the milk business was slow, I'd worked my way into a wet-wash laundry because I'd accept the lowest rate of pay that others refused. We were still riding out the depression, and over this period I'd worked for a landscape gardener, getting dropped off each morning at some opulent home to be bossed by the lady there; I'd helped build a greenhouse in Wayland; worked on farms in Weston and processed milk for Judge Hannon—who owned a farm run for his "lover" Tom. I considered all these people my friends, but suddenly I realized that I was in the midst of a nest of homosexuals. Feeling uncomfortable, I changed again.

Now with the laundry job less than satisfying, I was happy spending my free hours enjoying the Frenchman's hospitality. One afternoon he and I were sitting in the kitchen carrying on one of our usual, easygoing conversations. Florie joined us and the topics changed, but the talk remained simple, almost thoughtless. Suddenly, out of nowhere, the Frenchman looked up at me, smiled slyly, and asked, "How would a little chicken farm in the country strike you?"

I was surprised, but without thinking I said, "Fine." Right away I had a queer feeling that I was about to jump too quickly into something with one of my "I guess so" or a "It might be worth a try" answers. But once again my mouth went right ahead despite my mind's warnings, and within a few minutes Florie and I were engaged.

Within a few weeks we rented a small place in South Billerica, which made for a long daily trip through Lexington to the laundry in Waltham. I traded in my car for a half-ton pickup truck, and we moved out. In my spare time I rigged up the outbuildings for laying hens, and we sold eggs to some friends near Banks Square in Waltham.

The state hospital was right on my way to the laundry, so Florie kept on working there when she felt like it. But I never really liked that. I didn't trust her—by then I didn't really trust anyone. Too often I arrived home to find her combing her hair or straightening out the sofa cushions. I began to feel squeamish and nauseated all day at work. I lost a lot of weight and usually just couldn't eat during the day. The doctors thought it was the chemicals that were used in the wet-wash water and gave me medicines to coat the lining of my stomach. They helped some, but I still didn't eat much during the day. I'd often come home with a good healthy appetite, anticipating a nice hot dinner. But with increasing regularity Florie would be moody and distracted, turning aside my questions with complaints of a headache or tiredness.

A few weeks before our first Christmas together, I noticed some warm gloves on the front hall table. I decided they must be a present for me, but I didn't let on I had noticed them there. A few days later I drove into the yard just as the local grainman was driving out. All my frustrations and suspicions suddenly exploded. I burst into the house and immediately accused Florie of betraying my trust and her marriage vows. "How can you care so little for me?" I yelled. "I work all day and half the night just to give you a decent home. I come home

Snow

starving and you never have anything ready when I get here. You're nothing but a bitch, using our home while I'm away." She denied everything, but week after week it was consuming me with doubts.

After Christmas I saw the grainman wearing the gloves I'd seen in the front hall. Either Florie was too mad at me for doubting her, or she had always intended them for him. I never mentioned them to her, but questions kept gnawing at me. The mania for accusing her wouldn't leave me. I spied on her, trying to catch her in the act. I'd return home early, unexpected. Occasionally I'd make an excuse to go out late in the evening, then return sooner that I'd said. I never caught her, but my suspicions continued to grow until finally there was no peace in living. In less than two years together we were further apart that when we'd first met. We rarely spoke to each other and never showed any affection.

Finally we accepted the inevitable and settled on a divorce. I gave her all my possessions. I didn't care; I wanted out, and any price seemed a bargain at the time.

The Second Marriage and Divorce

10

Cora Clara Reappears

ROOSEVELT HAD TAKEN the country well out of the depression, but by 1937 the troubles in Europe were brewing and our recovery and jobs were the result of shipping supplies to France and England. Hitler's brownshirts were gathering in larger groups; troubles over there meant more work for us at home. Good and bad seemed to go together.

After leaving Florie, I found a driver's job at Anderson's Dairy and a cabin to go with it. With an airtight stove and a cot I was all set. I ate my meals at local diners and had friends who stopped in for beer in the evenings. I needed company and free drinks drew friends, but it didn't work out. I just couldn't get along with other young men. I soon let these friendships die out and devoted more of my time to old man Anderson. I'd give him a hand getting out to the pickup truck so we could take drives. The beer now went to him, as it was his last pleasure.

When I was alone on the streets young girls often approached me. Bold young women would come up Main Street after dark and try to get an affair started with me. Usually I spurned them; I just didn't feel any attraction. As in the past, I broke the day into two parts and caught a night's sleep by halves.

One day I learned that Mrs. Corliss, my ex-mother-in-law, was very ill in the Waltham Hospital. I got a phone call from a family friend who told me the old woman had been asking for me. I promised to be and asked her to meet me at the hospital.

I arrived at the hospital at two the following afternoon. A nurse showed me to the right room. Annie hadn't arrived yet, so I was nervous and not particularly looking forward to this meeting. I had no social training and had never been able to handle any new situation comfortably. I entered the room, clutching my cap in my hands. For a few moments everything seemed a blur, and all I could make out was Mrs. Corliss's drawn face smiling up at me from the bed. Her eyes kept moving from me to some other point in the room, and finally I noticed we were not alone. There was a young girl standing by the window—a beautiful girl with black hair and smooth, pale skin. I knew I'd never seen her before, but something in her face struck a chord of recognition within me.

"Come here," Mrs. Corliss said, beckoning to the girl. The old woman was smiling. "Cora," she said, "I want you to meet Snow Meader . . . your father." I guess I'd figured it all out before the old woman said anything, but it was still a shock to realize this girl was my daughter. Mrs. Corliss went on talking to Cora. "I know your mother told you Mr. Peacock was your father, but that's not true. She was trying to protect you, but I thought you should know the truth. Snow was your mother's first husband. Mr. Peacock didn't come along until after you were born."

The whole meeting was awkward, but Mrs. Corliss summoned the strength to keep things moving. Cora was standing by the bed, holding her grandmother's hand when Annie arrived. A nurse followed and stood just inside the door, keeping a close eye on her patient. Cora stared at me—a father she had never known until now. The old woman quickly filled in Annie on the long-kept secret. Annie nodded dumbly and responded with her usual stupid questions: "How are you feeling?" and "How's the food here?" The meeting was cut short when Mrs. Corliss waved everyone out of the room. She was satisfied that she'd done her duty. Outside the hospital Cora and I awkwardly said good-bye and went our separate ways, carrying our surprise and private thoughts away in silence.

A year later Cora Clara married and moved to Sudbury. I occasionally visited her there, and gradually we got over our surprise and self-consciousness. Mrs. Corliss was transferred to a state hospital and died a short time later.

Other than this unexpected reunion, my life remained on a fairly even keel. Sometimes I was lonely so drove out to see Annie in Natick,

Cora Clara Reappears

but it never worked out. First she had married a gifted man in Waltham and bore him five children before he died of delirium tremens. After another tough period on her own, she remarried, this time to a gentleman named Wheeler. I guess her new husband made her feel superior to me. Whenever I dropped by she'd greet me coldly and follow that up by berating me with cruel names. After a while she wouldn't even let me in the house.

Her rejection annoyed me, but I realized I'd just have to make out on my own. My situation really wasn't too bad. I was working steady, but anxious to be my own boss again. My desire to reach the top of something was still with me, so I set out to round up my old milk route customers. Things worked out well. I was in business for myself.

My milk business grew so fast that soon I'd saved enough to begin thinking about another farm of my own. This time the Federal Land Bank loaned me enough money to take over a large house and barn on 118 acres of land between Concord and Sudbury. A cattle dealer helped out with some additional cows and loaned me a young bull to keep them bred. What a day's work this made! To Sudbury to feed and milk my cows and put them out to pasture; back to Waltham to have the milk processed; load my truck; ice off the milk; cover my route and make my collections. At night I milked the cows and left that milking in the cooler until the following morning. It was weeks before I even looked into my new house. Luckily it was in good order, with a clean kitchen and bathroom, all freshly painted. But it was the hay and the pastures that I really wanted. There were two brooks, and water was pumped from a deep well to the house and barn.

I bought the place in 1940, and a year later the United States was at war. I received my draft notice and went down for my physical, which disgusted me—I hated having men look at me. I thought for sure I'd be taken, but between my cows and the drop in the age limit, I was never called. I settled back into my labor, bought a workhorse at an auction, and filled the hay bays in the barn for the coming winter.

11

The Black Market Years

FOR THE NEXT few years a family called the Bonners kept me up to my ears in trouble. They were customers of mine, one of the largest families on my route. Mrs. Bonner was the hardworking center of the family. Her husband worked every few days in a machine shop, but just lay around the rest of the week. There was an unmarried daughter, a married daughter with a small child, girl friends, in-laws, and grandchildren. Nobody ever seemed sure about how many supper places to set or how many beds to prepare. I thought their hospitality was natural and generous. What laughter—what a jolly mother—what coffee and doughnuts! The table was always covered with "boughten" cake and eclairs, candy, cookies, cheese, and crackers. Empty beer cans were found under the couch, the table, and the chairs. Mrs. Bonner was always greeting someone with a hug and a kiss. I was drawn to them and their life.

One day Mrs. Bonner told me they were being evicted. Without stopping to think, I said, "Why don't you drive out to my place in Sudbury. If the house is anything you could use, it might help out."

Out to Sudbury they went, and on their return they told me the house was perfect—ten rooms, a big kitchen, and a full bath upstairs. I accepted thirty dollars a month for rent. That didn't include the barns or the fields, since I needed them for my business.

As I was in Sudbury each day caring for my cows, I saw a lot of the Bonners. They were certainly informal, but I shut my mind to their doings. I enjoyed their personal greetings—the fuss they made over me removed some of my loneliness. I drank a lot of beer with them but never enough to slow down my heavy schedule.

During the war there was a great deal of cheating by people who wanted more gas, tires, meat, butter, or anything else rationed with stamps or just not available to the general public. Big dairies could get all the tires they needed, but small businessmen like myself, with only enough customers to fill one truck, were denied legal replacements. Never mind that we needed tires to stay in business, support ourselves, and serve the public; we just weren't big enough. I was forced to get my tires from a basement black market in Waltham. Heavy cream was rationed, but I could grab all I wanted where my milk was pasteurized. The people I knew thought these deeds showed smartness. No one ever mentioned right or wrong. We had to outsmart those who had come from homes like ours, but who were now in power positions against us.

The Bonners had a brother-in-law who had been a butcher. The whole gang thought my smaller barn would make a great slaughterhouse. "I suppose you could try it," I said after they had decided. All hands turned to putting in a water heater, a heavy rope-hung hook and some strong benches of table height. They destroyed an old blacksmith anvil and forge and threw away the old water barrel. Only the row of horseshoes strung along a wooden bracket was left as a reminder of earlier days. They put in a cement floor with a primitive drain in the center. I got no extra rent, but soon my lanes were crowded with cars and trucks coming and going day and night. A well-dressed man turned up from time to time, and Mrs. Bonner told me he was a government inspector, but my instincts told me this surely was a black market activity. Sometimes a rabbi would show up as well.

This ran along for some weeks, but it was out of my control and becoming a nuisance. The town officials were upset, and of course I was the one they blamed. Relations between me and the Bonners grew strained. They stopped greeting me and hid in the house whenever I was around. My real estate agent advised me to lock up the barn or risk losing it by default. I took his advice, but the Bonners retaliated by calling the county sheriff. A legal battle started. Mrs. Bonner tried to pretend she was on my side and "cousined" up to me. She and her daughters seemed to be sincere, but during these weeks

Snow

the locks were broken, the doors forced, and the buildings used during my absence. Finally the court closed them up. The outside members disappeared along with all the extra cars. It left me limp, but the Bonners stayed on, paid me my rent, and gradually brought me back into their lives.

Some evenings when I wasn't out at the Sudbury house, I was picked up again in Waltham by the old Frenchman, my ex-father-in-law. His other daughter, Arline, was at home now with her twelve-year-old daughter. Arline worked as a hairdresser on Moody Street. She was slender and had beautiful auburn hair. We went to a few veterans' functions with her father and had a grand time. We'd both been through a lot of hell and felt safe together. It wasn't love; it was a need. Her previous marriage had ended because of mistrust. We both felt that if we couldn't trust anyone else, perhaps we could be comfortable with each other.

She used to ride out with me in the afternoons to drive in the cows. She teased me about the house, still rented to the Bonners. She wanted to see the inside, but I wanted to keep her from meeting my tenants. I knew she'd probably end up fighting with the women. But by midwinter she'd pushed me into marriage and insisted that we claim the ell and live in the house after all. She fixed up a bedroom, a sitting room, and a kitchenette. We had to share the one bathroom, which was, at best, inconvenient. Arline's daughter was with us a lot, and I soon realized I had to support her, too. If I gave Arline money for food, I'd find it turned into a child's dress. I tried explaining that my income wouldn't cover any extras, but Arline didn't seem to hear. I found myself wishing the girl had stayed with her grandparents.

Mrs. Bonner was trying to be friendly again, but every night Arline accused me of all kinds of immoral actions with the Bonner family. I had to sit in my truck outside the hairdressers' when Arline was working because she didn't trust me out of her sight, even if I was with her father. She said she was afraid I might see some other woman there. At home there was no lovemaking; we fought all night.

Then Mrs. Bonner began dropping hints that she'd had twins by me—babies who hadn't survived birth. I was being torn to pieces by two women, each crazy jealous of the other. Life was impossible. I seemed to have two choices: put the Bonners out of the house or take Arline back to her father. The Bonners refused to leave peacefully. Arline agreed to return to the city life, provided I sell the cows and the farm. That seemed my only choice, so I went to a friend and he advertised the place for me in a Boston newspaper. There were im-

Snow's farm in North Sudbury and Concord.

mediate responses, and a number of people drove out to see the house and land.

I put all my extra time into painting the farm machinery and wagons. I sold the milk to a wholesaler who picked it up from the cooler.

I never left the grounds, as Arline wouldn't let me out of her sight. We continued to fight through the nights. More than anything, I was confused. All my life I'd seemed to climb and fall, climb and fall. Now things were falling down around me, and I couldn't seem to find a reason for any of it. The Bonners collected their things and were camping in the kitchen, but they refused to leave the house. They refused to let prospective buyers look at their part of the house. No one spoke to me. The doors were locked, and when an agent tried to get in Mrs. Bonner blocked his way.

In the middle of August two middle-aged women came out, following my agent's car. Arline and I were in the cow "linter." One woman gasped with pleasure, "Oh, June. What a wonderful place for saddle horses. Paddocks right by the barn, shade trees, pastures, hayfields. . . . And look at that dirt road for riding! It's not so very far from Newton. Can't we get this farm?"

The other lady spoke to me. She wanted to look inside the house to see if the old features were still there. This would be her home, and her furniture had to suit it. I told her about the Bonners, but she went right to the door anyway. She was apparently a lady who knew how to approach such a situation. Mrs. Bonner let her in immediately. The two ladies went over every inch of the house, then looked over the barns, the old workshop, the wellhouse, and the ox-shoeing building behind the house. The forceful lady made a list of everything as she went about. She sketched the whole layout and the floor plans, too. I showed her the underground passage between the ell and the barn. When I brought out a folder on the past history of the place, she was as excited as a child with a picture book. She borrowed the folder and made an appointment to return the next day. It seemed both she and her friend held positions in some health agency, working all day. They said they wouldn't be here until after five o'clock.

Some strange feelings were passing through my body. An entirely new change in life, I thought. Never will I look back. Right now, standing here in this sunny doorway with my wife of six months, I know this gentle but forceful woman will take some wonderful part in my life.

This woman, Mrs. Gale Whittemore, was living in her apartment with a friend, Ruth. They were both anxious to move out before winter set in. They returned the next afternoon and made their decision to buy. A real estate agreement was drawn up immediately for a quick sale. "Miss June," as I came to call her, was out almost every day, after that, making plans. The Bonners were told the place had been sold and miraculously disappeared almost over night. They rented a house down the road, so they weren't out of my life yet.

Arline was pleased and excited by the progress of things. We traveled back and forth to Waltham, visiting her parents. One day, shortly before the passing of the papers, we were driving down Route 117 when suddenly Arline began one of her tirades. She shot her anger at me with threats, ugly names, and accusations. Finally, just as we reached the city streets, she swung her heavy pocketbook across my face and I was forced to pull over to the curb. Before I'd even turned off the engine she was on me with her long fingernails, raking them down my face, clawing me like a lioness. Screaming and fighting, she opened the car door and practically fell out onto the sidewalk. "We're through!" she yelled. "I'm going to make you pay for all you've done to me."

She stomped down the street toward her family home. I turned around and drove back to Sudbury. There I washed my face and found blood had run down over my jacket. My eyes were swollen; the right side of my face was deeply cut. I spent the night alone. When Miss June came the next afternoon, I simply told her I'd had an accident and that Arline would be back. Miss June turned her car around and left without getting out.

Arline's brother came and emptied our apartment. He left me an oil stove, a mattress, and a few pans and a coffee pot. I'd hidden in the barn while he was there. When Miss June returned, she insisted I tell her the truth. She was a bit surprised and naturally worried because she didn't have full ownership yet and wondered if the sale might be delayed now. She and Ruth were planning to move right in and had already given notice to her landlady. She suggested I give her the Frenchman's address. I was glad to do it, because I surely didn't know what might happen next. Perhaps, I thought, this was the best way to find out.

Snow

Labor and love! there are no other laws
  To rule the liberal action of that soul
  Which fate hath set beneath thy brief control,
Or lull the empty fear that racks and gnaws;
Labor! then like a rising moon, the cause
  Of life shall light thine hour from pole to pole,
  Thou shalt taste health of purpose, and the roll
Of simple joys unwind without a pause.
Love! and thy heart shall cease to question why
  Its beating pulse was set to rock and rave;
  Find but another heart this side the grave
To soothe and cling to,—thou hast life's reply.
Labor and love! then fade without a sigh,
  Submerged beneath the inexorable wave.

"Labor and Love"
Edmund Gosse

The Black Market Years

12

Miss June

I WAS RIGHT. Miss June didn't let an hour go by before she started an investigation. It turned out she had been an agent for the Society for the Prevention of Cruelty to Children in Boston, and she certainly found out the whole history of Arline and her past acts. Later, she told me Arline had been married many times before. The events were always similar. She would stay married a while, then start a row, file for divorce, and take her husband's property. She generally was awarded enough from the court settlement to live for a number of years.

The day for passing papers came, so I had my real estate agent drive me to the office. We found the conference room full of people. Claims had been made against the real estate, so Miss June had to make out a whole list of checks. Arline was represented by her lawyer, her daughter, and a friend. The land bank had a representative there as well. The balance due the bank after the sale of the cows had been paid off. I owed a grain bill, a fuel oil bill, a mortgage, and a loan from the real estate agent.

A broken and confused man, I sat in a back corner with my head on my chest. No one spoke to me. For the first time in my life I was frightened. There was no fight or bounce left in me; empty, faraway thoughts filled my mind. I guess it was the unreality and impossibility of the scene around me. The sudden return to flat broke—this time worse than ever before, as I didn't even have a place to go—was more than I could take.

Just when my desperation was reaching its peak, Miss June came up and spoke to me. She and Ruth wanted me to stay on for a while until I found a job. They said I could have the ell apartment, and if I'd serve as a caretaker they'd keep me in meals. They offered to drive me back, but the agent had already made plans to do this, as he knew I had no car left now. I just couldn't have faced those women right then. I thanked them for letting me stay on; I couldn't wait to creep back to my dogs. I had a German shepherd and a fox terrier who followed me everywhere I went in my rooms, and, earlier, about the farm. Also, I still had a black workhorse, Jerry, who wandered around the fields and drank from the brooks. I did have an airtight stove, so I spent the rest of the day sitting on a box in the ell in Sudbury. The two women had gone for their day's work.

The next day Miss June's furniture load arrived. I'd brushed out all the rooms so they could spread out and get supper and spend their first night right in their new home. I hadn't eaten anything for two days and had spoken to no one since the agent dropped me off. I kept to my room when the movers arrived, just not having the courage to see anyone. Miss June seemed to accept my actions. She left a tray of food on the back stairs, and no one seemed to expect me to come down. The weekend passed this way. When they left for errands, I would take my dogs out, but as soon as I heard their car I'd run back upstairs.

Before they left for work on Monday morning, Miss June spoke to me from the kitchen. "Would you like to wash out the drawers in the pantry and set them out in the sun?" she asked. "And perhaps scrub the kitchen floor? The sink drain is slow; do see if the trap could be cleaned out. We'll be back at five-thirty." I found a good breakfast waiting for me, but I gave most of it to the dogs. I couldn't eat and hadn't slept very much either. I spent the day in the kitchen and the work filled my time and part of my mind. A very full tray was again left on the stairs, but again I gave most of it to the dogs.

The next day Miss June told me that Ruth's horse would arrive soon. "Would you fix up a stall in the small barn?" she asked. This was pleasant news and another day passed. If a car drove up to the house, I hid behind any building handy at the time. A private telephone was put in, but I never answered it. Each day some job was planned for me. I got my two meals a day, but never saw the womenfolk. Things

Miss June

went along like that for two weeks. I could stay in the kitchen, feed the horse, or take walks in the woods, but I never allowed anyone to see me. Life was going on, but neither the past nor the future was in my thoughts. I couldn't dare begin thinking about the recent past. I'd lost my Grammy when I was fourteen. Now I was forty-three, and the early, happy days on the Maine coast drifted back to me. I'd loved the sea, the old people in Boothbay, and all my earlier adventures. One morning I remembered the time I'd started out alone in a rowboat on a trip around some harbor island. The wind had changed suddenly, and I'd had to row for my life against the tide and the elements or be swept out to the open ocean. I'd learned a lot that day, and how I longed to get back there. But there seemed no possible escape from this odd sort of prison. I had fifteen hundred dollars in the bank, but I had no car, no home, and my health was breaking. My belt was drawn to the last hole. I didn't dare leave that dead-end road for fear of talk, criticism, and the "I told you so" that any friend or relative was waiting to throw at me. I couldn't understand these two women. They gave but asked for nothing.

Before Christmas they were joined by a young couple who had found no place to live after the ensign's separation from the navy in 1946. He worked for Arthur D. Little, while his bride, Jean, was a Simmons College graduate now working in Newton. Miss June's married daughter and her army husband joined the group, too—for the same reasons. He could not get an opening to return to college, and she was studying veterinary medicine at Middlesex College in Waltham. One more horse was added, which meant three, counting my Jerry. I made stalls for them, but when winter came in full force I let the girls sell my workhorse.

The financial arrangement was made within the group to keep monthly accounts and divide it all into equal parts. They agreed to carry my food cost between them, so I stayed on as before to take care of the farm and their animals. The daughter had two Welsh Corgis and a saddle horse. Ruth had her old gelding, and there were a couple of cats to keep the rats out of the grain. I shoveled late to keep the cars free of snow, kept the stable in top condition, swept and washed the kitchen ell, and kept three entrances cleared. They did the dishes and cleaned their rooms. I never went out of the ell into the main house.

All this time I was losing weight and thought my mind was going, too. I just couldn't get through all those terrible, lonely nights. I had to give my German shepherd away after he attacked the corgis and a visitor. Somehow, Miss June drew me out and got me to talk to her.

Snow

She soon discovered I had no furniture. It took her only an hour to remedy this. She must have held a tip-off meeting, for a week later I was called down by the navy man. He almost carried me downstairs and set me at the head of their dining table. It was a jolly crowd. I found the conversation quite unlike anything I'd ever heard before. The army boy was headed for courses in electronics—a new word to most people in those days. The navy boy was doing research on some kind of instant coffee powder. Miss June was a psychiatric social worker and child psychologist. Ruth was a Radcliffe College graduate and health educator. Sylvia was in her sixth year of college, becoming a doctor in veterinary medicine.

By midwinter, Jean had given up her nutritionist position for the city of Newton, as she was pregnant. She kept to her room in the mornings and came down to get dinner each night for the whole group. Ruth did the dishes; Sylvia had homework; Fred and Bob talked about the new products and the future in air flights, and developments in chemistry and radio, television, and such. All this talk, all this joking, all the goodwill and openness began to rekindle my hope. If these young people who had just come back from Germany and Japan could plan such bright and exciting futures, and if a person such as Miss June could understand this restless group and handle Ruth, who was a slightly depressed old maid, then certainly I could afford to take another look at life.

The rest of the winter passed this way. I regained my lost weight and spent weekends helping everyone. During their workdays I did bits of carpentry work, cared for their cars, did repairs, and painted inside and outside the house and the outbuildings.

Gradually Miss June taught me a lot about the old homestead. It had been built in the early 1700s and was once a self-sustaining farm. It had a long, attached workshop for the planning and production of stagecoach trunks. The original farm family raised and processed the cowhides, cut the lumber, made the iron hinges, and assembled the studded leather-covered wood trunks and hat boxes of all shapes and sizes. They had invented separate little tools for cutting and forming special corners of the patterns and had built drawers, holders, shelves, and cubbies to hold each item. Below the shop was a deep, granite-walled separate cellar containing a brick stove with a large cauldron for dipping sheep and hogs as well as for dyeing and processing wool and leather. From this room an eight-foot-high alleyway led

Miss June

to the basement of the present barn—which had been an ell to an earlier, larger cowbarn. Stairs led down to this tunnel and, after a hundred feet, led back up to the barn's main floor, or out a back access to the low fields and woods. Miss June showed me a disguised false board at the front edge of the hearth in the sitting room, near the original old kitchen. Under the board were two metal slides. Food had been handed down through this hole to escaping slaves, as this had been a "station" of the Underground Railroad used by abolitionists to help Negro slaves escape to the northern states and Canada.

One front room downstairs was lined with horizontal pine panels, very old and rich in color. The other had a dado and chair rail. The long room at the back of the chimney had one wall almost completely filled by a giant fireplace and brick oven. The dining room was the earlier bornin' room. Beyond that, in a large L-shaped addition, was the present kitchen, the woodsheds, storage rooms, and, far back, an outhouse. There were five fireplaces. Gunstock corner posts held the crossbeams, and wide floorboards covered each room. Miss June had furniture which she told me had been handed down to her through a long line of ancestors running back to the Mayflower's very first trip. The furniture certainly fitted this house, which I now found interesting and fascinating. Miss June looked up the history of the well, with its hand-drilled circular opening and shelf with drain—all from one piece of granite—and its enormous, elbowed wooden wheel overhead on which rope was rolled as the bucket was lowered and raised. The counterweight was a rock with a recessed groove that held its end of the rope in place. It turned out that Henry Ford had wanted this well for his Dearborn Museum. I was glad now that his agent had failed in his quest, for it made this farm a museum in its own right. The small building in the field outside the wellhouse held a pair of six-foot leather bellows, still in usable state. A complex series of wooden levers made it possible to pump air into the bottom of the firepit in the forge. Ox shoes were made here, and here the original homesteader's first field animals were shod with the necessary twin shoes.

Snow

13

Out Yet In Again

LATER THAT WINTER I overheard Fred complaining to Miss June and her daughter. "What Jean and I want to know," he said, "is why we have to pay a share for keeping Snow here. He doesn't do anything for us, as we can see, and we want our money for fixing up our own home." His words made me sick. I'd always hated young men, but nothing had happened all winter to trigger any reaction to these two. Now it had. I packed a few things and walked down the road to the Bonner house. I was once again made welcome with beer and kisses. The change in manner of living was a shock. I was swamped by their vulgarity, but I drank enough to remain sleepy most of the time. I was numb, as before, with no future. I felt a shame, but didn't recognize it at that time. I'd left Well-House Farm without explanation, and Mrs. Bonner prevented anyone from getting in touch with me.

By spring I heard that Fred and Jean had moved to an old house in Carlisle. Sylvia and Bob were to remain through part of the summer or until his college found a place for him. Finally a note got through to me. It was Miss June asking me to supper. I didn't answer but simply showed up. Fred had indeed left and things were quieter. I brought my clothes back and moved again into the ell.

My fox terrier had disappeared, so Miss June answered a local advertisement and bought me a lovely, tricolor collie-setter pup, Shep. He was a one-man dog but perfect for farm life; he never caused any trouble and proved to be a wonderful cow dog and a retriever of missing heifers; he was at my side or carrying out my orders. Miss June bought a female dog, much like mine, only smaller. Later, we raised puppies each year and sold them to pay for the dog food costs. She also bought an old workhorse so I could cut the grass and form it into haycocks. When they reached home, after work, the three of us built a load and hoisted the hay on a harpoon hay fork and mowed it away in the barn loft. Miss June also found two Tennessee Walking Horses so we could all take pleasure rides over our trails. Several times Sylvia and Ruth held riding parties with mounted couples joining in a good gallop over the brooks and through the pine groves. Miss June and Ruth had company over some weekends, and such guests often entered into the haying.

After Sylvia and Bob left for Durham, the three of us turned to the farming. We found a back way to the southern end of White's Pond in Concord and enjoyed many sunset swims in the clear water. I learned very little about the two women except that Ruth had been brought up on a farm and thought she knew a lot; Miss June had been everywhere and taught herself anything she wanted to know. She had hundreds of books and bought new ones on any subject of interest. She had been working on what she referred to as a master's degree at Boston University. At the end of the summer session, Ruth and I went to Symphony Hall to see Miss June, with a blue ribbon over a long black gown and a gold tassel on a square hat, receive her degree. There were very few women in the graduate school section, and it made me uncomfortable seeing her sitting with all those men. I was glad when it was over and we were on our way back to Sudbury. I'd never felt anyone was superior to me; I only accepted the fact that some people knew more than I did. Even on that question I was sure there were many things I knew better than most people.

During this season I never saw any of my friends or relatives. I had no mail except for a letter from Arline containing a ticket to some charity affair in Waltham. I knew she could want me back only because some recent scheme of hers had not proved profitable. Miss June suggested I ignore it, which I gladly did. A fortune-teller had told me my next wife would be a brunette, and Miss June and Ruth both had dark hair! While I was at the Bonners' I was teased considerably about this. But with Ruth and Miss June there was no talk of "affairs"—only work, their jobs, and animals. Miss June often asked me questions about myself. Where was I born? She seemed to enjoy

Snow

stories about the Maine seacoast when Annie and I were children there. I found myself proudly reminiscing about all sorts of details. Even after I told Miss June how badly Annie had treated me, she still thought I ought to go over to Natick to see her. She even agreed to go with me. I was surprised at how dignified and pleasant the call turned out to be. I was even more surprised when Annie started bringing her gang over once a week to spend an evening at Well-House Farm. She boarded state children to help out with expenses. Her husband, Mr. Wheeler, talked about old times in Lincoln, which lay between Sudbury, Concord, and Weston—where Miss June had been born. Her older daughters sometimes came along, but usually it was thirteen-year-old Clifford, her only son, who accompanied her.

Toward fall Annie asked Miss June to take Cliff for the winter and have him attend the Sudbury school. Annie told Miss June that she wanted Cliff out of their house because he disturbed everyone, especially his stepfather. So it came about that there were four members at the farm the following winter. Cliff learned to ride and took to the more cultivated life very well. With his fine blond hair, he really was a rather handsome boy. He had a dog that slept on the rug by his bed. He'd had his problems in life, but this was where Miss June could help. His mother had always hated him and had tried to send him away before. He knew he wasn't wanted. Miss June eventually became his legal guardian through a court order in Natick.

In the fall I grew restless again. The women were at work; Cliff was at school; and on two evenings a week Miss June attended night classes and didn't get home until ten o'clock. She was now working on a Ph.D., which had something to do with psychology. I really never knew what all those words meant, but I guess no one thought I didn't. We talked things over, and Miss June thought I might not be so lonely if I had a cow or two to fuss over. So I used some of my money to buy two Holstein cows. Later I rode with Miss June to a cow dealer and she picked out four more, which she paid for herself. A Concord distributor collected the milk, and my life picked up again.

Miss June slept downstairs in the paneled room, and brought her tea and toast to her room each morning before dressing for the trip to Newton. The rest of us slept upstairs in the main house. Cliff and I had small rooms at the back, while Ruth kept her large, sunny room overlooking the paddock and maples at the front. After the war few cars were available, as production was slow in making the changeover from guns and airplanes to pleasure vehicles, but Miss June did find an old Ford that actually ran—although it burned a lot of oil. She used the excuse that one car was not enough in case of an emergency. Someone else had always bought my cigarettes and done my errands. Now I could get out on my own again.

The hot-air, oil-fired furnace blew up one weekend, which meant firemen and then repairmen. I hated their intrusions and kept outside while the workmen were in the house. During the whole year I'd been telling Miss June stories about my boyhood. She had a collection of photograph albums, which we shared, but actually it was she who was filling out a picture of my early years. She even drove to Maine to look up my earlier homes and take pictures of the gravestones of my mother and grandmother. At home, Cliff would study and slip upstairs about nine; Ruth would eat an orange about ten o'clock and go to bed; Miss June and I would sit by the open fire and talk well into the night.

Part 3

Rescued

14

Is This Abyss Too Deep?

LET US LOOK BEHIND the scenes of this skimpy coverage of Snow's life to this point. In a general view of psychology, we'll select some ideas from various authors. This first group will be collected from Karen Horney's *New Ways in Psychoanalysis*. She suggsts that in considering the relation between culture and neurosis, only those trends matter which all have in common. A neurotic development in an individual arises ultimately from feelings of alienation, hostility, fear, and diminished self-confidence. It is basic anxiety or basic insecurity that necessitates the rigid pursuit of certain strivings for safety and satisfaction; failure to reach either or all may constitute the core of neurosis. Therefore, the first group of factors bearing on neurosis to be looked for in a given culture is the circumstances that create emotional isolation, potential hostile tension between people, insecurity and fears, and a feeling of individual powerlessness. The fact that our culture is built on individual competitiveness is probably why failure to succeed in this area causes potential hostility and therefore ranks as first cause of further neuroses. Economic and social success are necessary for security. Disturbances in interpersonal relations, resulting in isolation and repeated retrials at forming permanent relationships, is cause enough for breakdown. Lack of solidarity in this area may result in loss of self confidence. This is a great test of emotional strength. A child is taught that people are well intentioned toward him, that it is a virtue to confide in others, and that to be on one's guard is almost a moral defect. This was our boy when he left Boothbay Harbor after his Grammy had died in his arms.

Snow's experience on Fiske Avenue, where he was abused, exploited, beaten, lied to, suspected, and belittled in the social world led to his neurotic conflicts. These, of course, were fed by concern with the incompatible strivings for safety and satisfaction that could not be found in his present house. He had to search particularly for cultural ways outside his uncle's home for this safety and satisfaction. He needed to present himself for approval and acceptance in a group that would appreciate his honesty and unselfishness. Persons who have succumbed to a neurosis are those who have been more severely hit by the existing difficulties, particularly in their childhood.

Though Cora Clara Meader McKenney did have three babies born to her, she must have contracted the tuberculosis very early in her marriage. Millworkers were susceptible through two corridors in that period. The actual working hours were long in themselves, exposing a group in close proximity with its members. If they stopped at a local beer parlor on the way home, these men stood or sat hanging together in a sunless, unhealthy place. Mugs were certainly not sterilized! At home it was even worse; some older member was probably incapacitated by chronic tuberculosis, living in a corner of the kitchen or even handling the food and the babies. The mill housing was stretched along the rivers where they huddled together above the spray of the dirty waters. Some people developed an immunity to the germs; others had childhood lung spots causing colds with catarrh and often bronchitis. If these young people moved away, they probably escaped a later full-blown case and nothing but an x ray would discover the controlled infection.

Cora Clara had no such immunity and, being nightly exposed to a shower of germs, quickly succumbed to "galloping consumption." Snow, being the first child, was tenderly cared for, particularly by a possessive, visiting grammy. The second child died; the third would miss knowing her mother at all. The two surviving children were hustled out of their home into the arms of an adored, maternal grandmother Meader and spent some solid, healthy years on a sunny hill overlooking the salt water. Unconsciously, Snow must have felt that his father had abandoned him. The father was still alive even though Snow hardly realized what the death of his mother meant as a state of being. They both forsook him. He had between seven and eight years of the firmest, surest type of security: a home, love and care, and the financial comfort of the times. Again, a completely misunderstood abandonment took place. His grammy drifted away without any warning, advice, or assurance for a future course. She, too, forsook him. The lovely colored will had spoken a lie. The dreaded uncles had their way, and Snow spent thirty years reaching around in the dark seeking a mother, or a grandmother—"Gar take Gar boy,"—or simply a home with enough food to eat. He discovered too late that his mother had unwittingly left him; that Grammy had expected to live longer but had left two important things undone, one good and one bad. The first was the fact that in stealing the children she probably saved them from tuberculosis; the second was her failure to register her will. Even Judge Kenniston's office seemed to have had no copy, even though she outlived him. The traumas and the dramas of Snow's first sixteen years were a built-in foundation for the development of paranoid symptoms.

The following ideas are based on statements found in *A Handbook of Psychiatry* by Lichtenstein and Small. The former was in charge of psychiatry and legal medicine for the district attorney, New York County; the latter, an instructor at Cornell Medical College.

They agree that the onset of paranoid reactions occurs most often after the age of thirty. Men are afflicted more often than women. To be sure, many of our beliefs may be nothing more than rationalizations of our desires, but when these convictions are subjected to the test of reality and found wanting, we are able to give them up. However, paranoid individuals tenaciously cling to their convictions and, if questioned, will even further elaborate them. Such people have acceptable behavior in other areas. If a man with a paranoid tendency also shows indications of exaggerated depression, then there is grave risk of suicide. Treatment of such people is difficult, and results are most discouraging. If an acute crisis arises, the problem comes to the surface. Snow, in this biography, becomes physically weak; an opening in his guard was recognized; and a trained person could pick up the syndrome at that point. No one else had the slightest hint that he had a mental aberration. Without this understanding, professional friend, he would either have taken his life; he would have been placed in a mental hospital for such an attempt; or his delusional fears would have caused a collapse, in which case he might have welcomed the security of a hospital.

As it fortuitously turned out, such a person was at hand and the farm in the Sudbury-Concord woods was an island of safety. Snow had a tangle of twisted beliefs that almost belied straightening. But by cutting back life to its simplest needs, and working for accepted premises, a beginning could be made. Many crossroads were met, but never a dead end.

This last book, which is used for reference, is called *Psychiatry for Social Workers* by Lawson G. Lowrey, M.D. By chance this book was published by the Columbia University Press in 1946, the year when Snow met Miss June. Its contents had not been applied immediately to the situation when Well-House Farm was purchased from Snow, because he, having no home at that moment, had not acted in any than a self-controlled manner. No one would have any recourse than to let him seek his own salvation. But he was quiet and sober with a sad appeal that seemed to cover a quite different personality. It was obvious that he could have been led up or down as long as someone spoke to him with any interest. Our offer of home and meals was enough.

Snow had gone to his sister with some of his special possessions they locked up in a henhouse. This was during the period before the papers were passed and he was distraught. She lectured him about his indecent wife, his foolishness, his past history of mistakes. She told him he was crazy. Later he returned for his things, but she had let her children break into the building and take anything they wanted. This time he had no car and had to walk many miles to buses running from Natick and Waltham to Maynard back to Sudbury. His mood became depressed to the edge of oblivion. His intellectual ability seemed to shrink, and his faith in his judgment had almost evaporated. He was ill without realizing it. He thought his luck was gone—that's as far as his thinking went.

Dr. Lowrey wrote a warning in his book. Anyone attempting to help such a personality would probably find a patient with little ability to maintain a successful personal relationship with anyone for any length of time. He will blame his own failures and errors on anyone or anything. Never argue with a paranoiac. Just listen and agree until you find some obvious example for proof against his inaccurate conclusions. If you can get him to accept even part of an error in his viewpoint, then, with the stretching of your patience, this little opening may be widened.

There are ideas of suspicion, jealousy, conviction that a spouse is unfaithful; ideas of persecution are always present in some degree. Freud thought there was an inversion of a homosexual mechanism due to some failure to identify with the correct parent or the lack of chance to transfer affection from mother to a loved bride. He fights to

expose his heterosexual ability even though he is less than a successful lover. He is apt to turn "she loves me" into "she hates me."

A paranoid person often needs financial assistance and social supervision as he starts out to reevaluate his life. He will need the emotional support of one person over a long period of time—better one of the opposite sex. One slip and the worker can lose rapport- —and the case. Success is seldom achieved. Patience and steadfast- ness are attributes of a good social worker, as well as friendship.

As an employed professional psychiatric social worker, nothing could be more interesting than the challenge of an attractive new acquaintance. Everyone called him Snow. Some neighbors and friends called him Mr. Snow, not realizing that he had a surname. To this day, anyone having business or social connections with him quite naturally calls him Snow. This word "naturally" probably re- flects his manner toward anyone. He has an even temperament, almost entirely without self-consciousness; if he has the courage to meet anyone, he acts entirely on a surface relationship. He takes things as they appear to him, and others never look for hidden meanings in his words. He either handles everything in a direct way, or he turns away from it entirely.

When Ruth and I decided to find a farm, within commuting dis- tance to Newton and Boston, we each had our own reasons for getting away from postwar situations. I, as executive secretary of a Newton health agency, had hired Ruth as an approved health educator. She had added special courses at Simmons College to prepare herself and was, obviously to me, trying to overcome a tendency to withdraw socially but recognized, at thirty-two, she should try to mix with people and maybe even find a woman companion or a husband. I, quite obviously, was not marriage-bound, having spent twelve years finding an important place where substantive satisfactions would fill my future. A disappointing marriage had conditioned me to find my own salvation. Neither of us had good looks, only honest, good intentions. She wore formal clothes only while on the job; I changed from newer back to older when at home. She purchased her coats and dresses, while I sewed or concocted mine. We both had limited incomes, but I did have property and private resources. We both could talk and make conversation, but she could fall asleep at a meeting or the dinner table, while I had trouble falling to sleep after I had crawled alone into bed. I carried burdens on my mind that she didn't seem to possess at all—which might be a worrisome, understood concern for others. Her life had put her into a rut—mine certainly had not. She had men, as such, on her mind, while I met men, women, or children on an equal-interest basis. It had been my life's ambition to hold a formal position, and I had spent forty years toward fulfilling this wish, studying and practicing to earn degrees covering remedial work; tests and testing; clinical psychology; as well as straight teaching, tutoring, and finally social work. Because I had taught in private schools, I was able to attend classes in late afternoon or night while working on concurrent days.

Snow attracted the attention of us all. He had an unusual personality. Though not tall, he had a straight, handsome look. Sitting, he was a large man: large features, large chest expansion, large hands, and a sturdy look. Standing, he had short legs with shapely ankles and a size nine shoe. His eternal caps were wool in winter, whipcord in summer—an identification that made many of us exclaim wherever we were, "Isn't that Snow?" and any of us would turn or rush to the window. Of course we would know it couldn't be he in Boston or in a store or on a trolley, but anyone in our office, or anyone having met him, kept seeing him in imagination.

He had humor. With a one-line, economical remark, he used to explain a condition or sum up a conclusion. As he grew more relaxed at Well-House Farm, he had many of us laughing. He saved some awkward situations and delighted guests and members. We referred to these as "Snowisms." They weren't puns or jokes, more like aphorisms, American-made Chinese proverbs, or "Confucius say . . ." They would not stand alone; they were not repeated story-line jokes, just off-the-tongue remarks that fit their particular situation or point of conversation then going on. They were original and seemingly without forethought or plan—just a grouping of words that drew everyone together in a healthy, liberating manner. If some person ended with "by George," and his name happened to be Henry, Snow would synchronize, "and Henry, too." We often quoted them, but they did not live on paper or long in our memories, I'm now sorry to say. At a boring meeting, sitting on folding chairs, I on his left, a woman knitting at his right, one speaker was fumbling for words during a drawn-out speech. Snow's low whisper to me could be heard along the row. "She'll have that sweater finished at this rate." Everybody near us recrossed his legs and giggled with bent head.

Snow

On a later occasion, we were dining out one Thanksgiving Day with but one outsider at the table. He was a middle-aged man from Scotland doing exchange work in psychology at Harvard Graduate School. I knew nothing of him. Family parties, held at great intervals, can be rather stiff affairs. There is at once too much to say, particularly of the past, and too much of the present to catch up with over a period of two hours. An outsider can foil all attempts from old or young. Into one of these blank spots Snow said quite clearly, "Do you know what an Aberdeen dinner is?" Our host-cousin looked surprised; his wife looked ashamed and apologetic; the college-aged young didn't have any answers either—but the guest broke into a roar of released laughter. Snow had contributed nothing to the conversation before this query, and his hosts couldn't cover their embarrassment. They had always thought of Snow as an ignorant, rather slow fellow. Indeed, the Scotsman was the only one with an answer. All turned to him. As we sat there with stretched stomachs from an American turkey dinner, it was Snow and this foreign guest who saved the day. "You run around the table and kick the cat!"

Another extraordinary ability belonging to Snow was his memory for details. He knew nothing of music and musicians, books or writers, but miles away from home in distance or time he would suddenly say, "Around the next right turn you'll find that old yellow house with the leaning remains of a windmill." There it would be. He couldn't follow a timetable or a roadmap, and never knew which fork to take at a break in the road. I always knew whether I was traveling north or south; he, never. But he would tell me what I would find while I was finding it.

One fall day we drove up our lane and parked outside the wall under the beech tree. Ruth ran into the house while I headed for the barn. Snow should have been milking the cows, but he hadn't stepped to the door to greet us. To my horror, I found him lying along the walk behind the cows. The three-legged metal stool was overturned. The milking machine was still pumping the suction cups on a cow's udder. I quickly switched off the motor, removed the rubber inflators, and unslung the kettle that hung on a leather strap about that cow's body. I set the stool aside because of its exposed, sharp legs. Then I leaned over Snow. I roused him enough to answer my question. Recognizing the condition as the consumption of alcohol, I pulled him

Is This Abyss Too Deep?

Snow in Well-House Farm, Sudbury, 1946.

Snow

onto his feet. With a quickly mobilized plan, I thought I might get him through the kitchen and upstairs before Ruth appeared. She would take her time changing and probably leave for the stable through the side door. Sharply, as though speaking to a child in a dangerous situation, I talked Snow along the path close to the house and somehow snapped commands that kept him moving. I pushed him right up his stairs, off the kitchen, and covered him after I had put him into a comfortable position on his bed and removed his shoes. I met Ruth outside and told her Snow was not feeling well, so we wouldn't set his place at the table that evening.

Later I went back to the barn and gave the cows hay and water and closed up things for the night. The overt action, which I had long expected, had now begun. I knew, deep down, that I was so very much involved I would have to keep on no matter how complicated my personal situation became. Somehow, he would have to count on me.

There was no chance of speaking to him again that night. I chatted with Cliff and Ruth as usual. Later, at Ruth's concerned insistence, I went up to check on Snow's condition. It almost had to come from her, because I alone knew of his true state and I would not have her know my personal concern. He was still asleep.

We were off as usual in the morning, and there was only time for a short aside: "Try to get through the day and we'll have a good chat tonight." On our return everything was in excellent order and Snow ate a fine dinner. I was almost too gay, but no one noticed. In the evening we talked for at least two hours. He said he had been upset and gone down the road for a bottle of wine. He left it in his room, but made the trip back and forth all afternoon taking tiny sips. He finished the last while he was milking and remembered nothing of our encounter the afternoon before.

To every question asked, he answered, "I don't know."

What had happened; what bad news had he had; who had been there; how had he felt; what had we said or done to upset him? He sat in the large wing chair and found no words of explanation. He really didn't seem to know. I wasn't satisfied at all. He was hiding everything from me.

For some time now we had chatted about his earlier, happier days. He had told me many details of his childhood that make up the first chapters in this biography. Now we had to find a connection between past and present and bring some subconscious thoughts to the surface. He could not see any reason why his behavior or his bad luck in

Is This Abyss Too Deep?

his relations with women could have any basis other than that they were untrustworthy and unfaithful and he was always correct in being suspicious of them. They had all brought the men into his home and had sexual relations with them. He couldn't accept any other solution to the break in each marriage.

I had tried to relieve his mind about any guilt on his part in the case of Arline. He readily agreed that she was "sick in the head." She couldn't even go into a store without dragging him along. She accused him of picking up girls, or of wanting to slip away to one, day or night. He could see her problem but never would admit he suffered from the same delusions.

In my major effort to restore his ego and unreasonable wounded pride, I just had to make him believe that he had not suffered a loss or been tossed aside—that there had been no love to lose, so he didn't have to suffer because of her leaving him.

The day I had driven to Lyman Street, to inquire for her health, I had a simple plan. It would make an excellent opening act. Arline's mother let me in with chatty cordiality. Her motives were to make sure the sale of the Sudbury farm would go through so her daughter would collect her share. I could see an old man sitting in the kitchen at the end of a long hall, but I did not meet him. I was shown into a front parlor. On a sofa, dressed in a shiny rayon housecoat was the "lady" in question. She was half buried in the marabou trim around her neck and her red-hennaed hair was carefully pinned to the top of her head. A cold compress was across her forehead, and one arm hung down from her side toward the rug. Her mother hovered about as though she expected her to faint again or possibly die at any moment. The sordid story of Snow's behavior, the cruel disappointment in her marriage, and her serious condition were all hastily exploded into my ears. Arline's weak voice could only convey half sentences interrupted by a series of groans.

Using interviewing techniques and a series of subtle questions, I pretty well pieced together their planned story. Arline had jumped out of the car and gone straight to the nearest telephone, not for a doctor, but rather for her lawyer. He called at her parents' home, followed by the doctor. The second gentleman would corroborate the lawyer's subsequent testimony when he filed Arline's complaint for a divorce.

Snow

Ha! I noticed that the cloth had fallen from the brow; there were no scratches or cuts, only a beautifying makeup from chin to hairline. The cloth was dry! So I pressed on, showing only sympathy and apparent acceptance. Over the sofa was a commonplace colored print of Venice or a Grecian shrine to a Vestal Virgin—or the like. Glancing at the other walls first, I let my eyes fasten on this frame. I exclaimed, "What a pretty picture—the colors are lovely in this room! Who painted this? Is it in Italy or Greece?" The prone, languid woman jumped to her feet, turned around to face the picture, and began to tell how they happened to own it. She leaned over the sofa with one hand on its back in an effort to read the signature. The ruse had worked better than at any time I had tried it before! But the poor woman realized what she had done and fell back across the sofa moaning. Her mother rushed over to help her re-drape the pink feathers and replace the masking cloth across her eyes.

I apologized for upsetting them all, wished them better health soon, and left. Well, I had their scheme tied down in my mind and a solid story to tell Snow. He need not feel guilt about his treatment of his wife. I should have seen his lawyer and helped him keep his money and furniture, but who would have expected a local judge not to see through the rigged marriage of six months' duration, and the contrived ending, as a connivance to rob Snow; making a living out of a string of such shortlived relationships, especially as they had all taken place in Waltham.

Snow felt pretty silly for having been fooled so easily, but he believed my version and admitted that actually they both suffered with the same jealous temperaments. He knew he had not loved her, but he had thought himself old enough to make a final try for companionship. "She was crazy," he admitted, but he still could not see that his behavior was anything but reasonable. Especially, he could see no similarity to his marriage attempts of the past. The divorce went through without his presence. His lawyer played both sides and let Snow down to the bottom. In Massachusetts, this then meant a six-month wait followed by two years more as a punishment of the guilty partner. In Snow's case, this circumstance rekindled his feelings of persecution and slowed down his recovery considerably. A gentleman allows the wife to file for the divorce; for Snow, he should have reversed that sequence as Arline attacked him and left his room and board that he had provided in a fine home.

These added pieces of broken pride were pressed deeper into the

Is This Abyss Too Deep?

morass of crushing episodes, making up his life, that now became an added part to his subconscious hurt. Because this had never been aired or explained, my job became even more complicated.

Shortly after the conclusion of his legal settlements, he went through another drinking day. Apparently he knew someone within walking distance who made strong wine. His method was always the same. He did not sit with a glass and drink it all down at once, but made a series of trips from the farm jobs to his room for one glass, then back down the stairs and out again, and so on. As each dose wore off, he'd repeat the ritual until he and the wine were through. I covered up for him somehow. Either Ruth stayed at work or Cliff was playing with friends; always some circumstance saved us both for another day and another try.

This unforeseen change in behavior worried me in many ways. It frightened me. What disturbed me was what might turn up next in such a sequence. I searched my experiences and my textbooks. Would Snow turn in upon himself with a new or a renewed confusion ending in complete discouragement, or would he turn outward with blame and harm to someone along his road of trials? One thing was clear to me—he should not be left alone for long periods. I stretched my lunch hour and drove home each day. On one such day two paperhangers had at last arrived to do over the living room. Snow was in hiding, but I found him in the barn. I put him into my car and drove over a woods road, out of sight of the house. He kept a closed mouth. White lines, which often appeared across his face, were wide and tight. Finally he broke his silence and blurted out his belief that I had been coming home at noon in order to keep a date with a paperer!

Now I knew how things stood. They were tense, unchanged, and fearful. The immediate course was to stay close to him until the men had left the job. Words had been wasted; extended, consistent actions on my part would be a requirement. Was he an alcoholic showing jealous reactions? Did he feel he was impotent? Was he depressed to the point of suicide? Should he be admitted into a hospital, or would he meet a psychiatrist by appointment?

15

The Chaos Before the Creation

FRIDAY AFTERNOON arrived at last. The four of us generally went shopping in Maynard, had a bite to eat, and attended an excellent motion picture at the Little Art Theatre. Snow seemed natural again, and certainly Ruth and Cliff had noticed nothing out of the ordinary all week.

After the cows were cared for on Saturday, I drove Snow back to Maynard to buy an outfit just for him. We had joke names for this or that: to me the technician from the breeding farm was "The Artificial Man," because he bred our cows; the army-navy-type store was named "The Ideal Clothing Store," therefore, the owner was "The Ideal Man." So, we visited The Ideal Man, who knew we called him by that name, and we laid aside item by item a complete outfit for Snow. Shoes, his choice of socks, colorful boxer shorts and white T-shirts, sport shirts, work trousers, a jacket, a lined topcoat, and a suit. Caps? Yes, but he wouldn't consider a hat! The Ideal Man created a New Man. Snow looked the part; now I hoped it would help him to become one. He liked browns, which are sad colors to me, a mark of a person who has given up hope; a women becomes the spinster, the man staid and unemotional. I teased him into greens and blues. His hazel eyes seemed browner over the greens, and his hair looked darker surrounded by the blues.

A few weeks passed, but still Snow had repeated his wine-sipping two or three times, if only to help him to sleep. I was earnestly trying

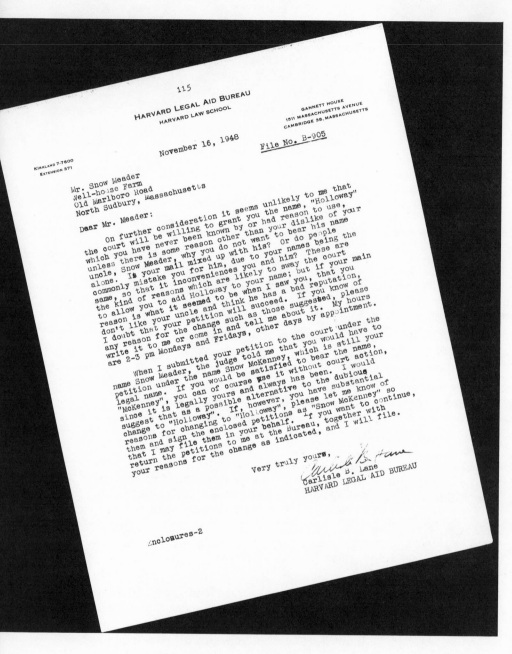

115

HARVARD LEGAL AID BUREAU
HARVARD LAW SCHOOL

GANNETT HOUSE
1511 MASSACHUSETTS AVENUE
CAMBRIDGE 38, MASSACHUSETTS

November 16, 1948   File No. B-905

KIRKLAND 7-7600
EXTENSION 371

Mr. Snow Meader
Well-house Farm
Old Marlboro Road
North Sudbury, Massachusetts

Dear Mr. Meader:

On further consideration it seems unlikely to me that the court will be willing to grant you the name, "Holloway" which you have never been known by or had reason to use, unless there is some reason other than your dislike of your uncle, Snow Meader, why you do not want to bear his name alone. Is your mail mixed up with his? Or do people commonly mistake you for him, due to your names being the same, so that it inconveniences you and him? These are the kind of reasons which are likely to sway the court to allow you to add Holloway to your name; but if your main reason is what it seemed to be when I saw you, that you don't like your uncle and think he has a bad reputation, I doubt that your petition will succeed. If you know of any reason for the change such as those suggested, please write it to me or come in and tell me about it. My hours are 2-3 pm Mondays and Fridays, other days by appointment.

When I submitted your petition to the court under the name Snow Meader, the judge told me that you would have to petition under the name Snow McKenney, which is still your legal name. If you would be satisfied to bear the name, "McKenney", you can of course use it without court action, since it is legally yours and always has been. I would suggest that as a possible alternative to the dubious change to "Holloway". If, however, you have substantial reasons for changing to "Holloway", please let me know of that I may file them in your behalf. If you want to continue, return the petitions to me at the Bureau, together with your reasons for the change as indicated, and I will file.

Very truly yours,

Carlisle B. Lane
HARVARD LEGAL AID BUREAU

Enclosures-2

The discouraging letter of November 16, 1948.

Snow

to decide what to do. Cliff and Ruth could not be brought into the problem. Cliff should think highly of his uncle; Ruth thought of him in romantic terms. He and she were both products of farm and country life, which gave them a wide area of common interest. But from my point of view I was playing a dangerous game with the welfare of us all.

To pursue the personal concentration on Snow, which was my best weapon to probe his inner conflicts, I began to trace back through his genealogy. He had no birth certificate, which, I found, accounted for his inability to seek town or state aid at any time. Over a period of two years we spent hours and days on research. First I wrote letters of inquiry to the town clerks of Topsham, Brunswick, Augusta, and others for facts on the Meader family. We corresponded with offices of vital statistics. We learned a few facts: one was that his Grammy Meader had never formally adopted the children, so their name should not have been Meader all those years. He couldn't remember his father's full name, but we put down various versions and received information that such a man had lived in Topsham. We also ascertained that Annie, or Angelia Isobel McKenney, was listed as the second child born of her parents. That helped to show Snow was probably the first. We drove to the cemetery in Brunswick to take pictures of the gravestones. Cora Clara had married a McKenney. Angelia's sons had put up only a small stone for their mother! In 1911 she had had set up a large memorial to her precious daughter, Cora Clara.

In answer from Mrs. Robinson, librarian of The Hubbard Free Library, of Hallowell, Maine, I learned that a man was doing research at that library on the Hallowells of Maine. She thought that he might know something of Snow's maternal grandmother through her maiden name. We wrote this gentleman, Everett Hall Pendleton, in New Jersey, and received a prompt answer, and excited response! He was compiling a volume on the "Old Colony Holloways," original proprietors of Taunton, Massachusetts, 1637.

To turn the sand back in the hourglass of Snow's years, we decided to follow up the idea of starting him over again; getting him to relive his boyhood; settling on a new name to give him a chance to excise those horrible middle years and start afresh. He had had to sign his name S. Meader, Jr., ever since he was fifteen. His uncle was Snow Meader. But because of this, Snow hated his own name as he hated

The Chaos Before the Creation

that man; therefore, he used only the S—his uncle insisted on the "Junior," as he disliked being confused with his nephew. The Waltham family called him Snowden, and his sister used to call him the Snowie. Of course his legal name had always been Snow McKenney, but he never knew that before our investigations. This put a lovely new light in his personality. I was particularly excited over these disclosures and rushed to make some arrangements for settling on a self-chosen name and having a proper birth certificate filed. We suggested the Hallowell because it was on his mother's side of his birthright. His distant cousin, E. H. Pendleton, made a good point for using the "Holloway" as it had originally been brought over from England in 1637.

To save costs, we drove to Harvard Square to use the resourses offered by the Harvard Law School. Seniors in that division were doing practice work and could research legal affairs for a small fee. Before any paper reached finality, it was checked by an instructor. First came the interview; then the papers were made out; and finally the date was set for a court appearance. All this took a number of trips back and forth. As the day drew near, we checked those papers only to find that our young "lawyer" had not thought that the name should start with the McKenney to be changed to Holloway! He had inserted "Meader" instead. All this wasted time had passed. When we brought this to his attention, his mentor sent word to us that his advice was for us to leave things as they were.

Well, this was not the idea at all. Snow couldn't take personal setbacks, particularly as this one formed another situation in which a young man was involved who had failed him. We then did what we should have done in the first place. We called my family's law office in Boston for an appointment. It was at this time that we drove to Temple, New Hampshire, to meet my parents. They were retired and were living in a beautiful, original saltbox house. They owned many acres, a few animals, and had a couple to look after the whole household. Father still rode his flea-bitten gray horse and kept another for guests.

We drove into Town the following afternoon, and a kindly, white-haired man thought the story was fascinating. He agreed with us all the way through it. This time he turned over the correct information to a young associate, and we were called to an early court hearing in Cambridge.

Snow

Snow was excited and a bit nervous. The first encounter had fizzled in his face, and he had no self-faith with another man. But, after we had chosen one of his new neckties and matching socks, he came back downstairs with renewed hope, dressed in the suit and coat bought from the Ideal Man. Our attorney met us in the corridor, and we were ushered right into a courtroom. Cases such as this were put ahead of the morning's list. We were placed in the front row so the judge could talk to us from there.

"So, you want to change your name. Why?"

"You see, Your Honor, I didn't like my uncle who had the name of Meader, so I thought I'd rather take my grandmother's maiden name. When we came to look it up, we found it should have been Holloway, not the Hallowell as it had been used since the 1700's."

"Where did you come from?"

"You know, Your Honor, I was brought up in Boothbay Harbor where . . ."

The judge leaned forward and said, "My clerk came from there!" At this point, he injected an introduction. "He still spends his vacations in the area and I've been down fishing with him." A brisk chat took place about the old town and its earlier years. Snow was getting the friendly acceptance we couldn't have hoped for in the solemnity of a large, nearly empty court. Our young lawyer relaxed, for he knew his part was successful. The judge signed the necessary papers while he talked. An outsider would have thought this was a reception or anniversary party being held in recognition of Snow's achievements. He was wished happiness and good luck. It was obvious that the judge enjoyed those moments, as his day would be filled with divorce cases and neighborhood quarrels. All the way back to Sudbury, Snow reminisced about his youth, and he was at least temporarily reborn into his gay, unworried boyhood. We gained insight to add to the mental portrait we had been drawing. Usually we had to press hard to get a drop of color—but on this day we had a stream to work into the fabric.

Some weeks later, a most difficult afternoon developed. We'd had visitors who had wanted to see the old farm and to investigate the underground tunnel, the old well wheel, the ox shoes and bellows. The group split and wandered all about the buildings and even up to the sugar bush and pine-bordered lanes to see the brooks. That night the white band had reappeared across Snow's handsome face. His

The Chaos Before the Creation

Form T-1

RECORD OF A BIRTH

Place of Birth _Topsham, Maine_

Street _____ No. _____

Child's Name _Snow McKenney_

Date of Birth _April 16, 1903_

Sex _M_ Color _W_

Living or Stillborn _____

No. of Child, 1st, 2nd, etc. _1st_

No. of children of this mother now living _____

Father's Name _Horace C. McKenney_

" Color or Race _W_ Age _21_

" Birthplace _Lisbon Falls, Maine_

" Residence _Topsham, Maine_

Street _____ No. _____

Father's Occupation _Mill Worker_

Mother's Maiden Name _Cora Clara Meader_

" Color or Race _W_ Age _19_

" Residence _Topsham, Maine_

" Birthplace _Boothbay Harbor, Maine_

" Occupation _Housewife_

Name and address of Physician (or other person) reporting said birth _Mrs. G. Dale Whittemore_ M.D. _Member Am. Assn. of Social Welfare_

Date when received by Town Clerk _Jan. 15, 1949_

State of Maine

I hereby certify that the above birth record is correct to the best of my knowledge and belief.

Alice R Merriman

Clerk of _Topsham, Maine_

over.

This record taken from affidavit sworn to and signed by Mrs. E. Dale Whittemore of North Sudbury, Mass., before Herbert Webster Martin Notary Public

Jan. 12, 1949

Snow's birth certificate. . . authenticated January 15, 1949.

Snow

eyes were almost yellow with sullen, suspicious warning. On my return from work on Monday, I found an excuse to get away from the house by driving over to Wayland to look at a cow that might be bought. We went in Snow's postwar, smoky car. While driving along a back road, he suddenly poured out a torrent of ugly words.

"You're only a whore, just like all the rest. You carried on yesterday and I could see you making a date. Where are you going to meet him?" I made a feeble attempt to stop him, but he wasn't listening. He was completely engulfed in the manufacture of this fiction and talked like one possessed of a well-thought-out story. He included past encounters, spoke of the uselessness of all the tricks I had tried to fool him with, of his knowledge of hidden secrets held from him. I couldn't stop this verbalization. But somehow this, too, was packed with vital information. It went too far. I was frightened now and I was furious. I'd had my fill of placating, listening, and helping. I reacted as an ordinary, decent woman would. I demanded to be let out and said: "I'll walk home."

I did walk for a while, but my legs were wobbly. He didn't let me get far before he came alongside and ordered me back to my seat. We drove without any friendliness.

This horrifying event brought me to the point of making a major decision. Recognizing a serious neurosis in him, possibly a psychosis—for at forty-five this process would be almost nonreversible—I felt I would have to either turn him over to a public alienist or move out of reach myself. I accepted the fact that I had, in undertaking a case outside the framework of an agency caring for such personalities, broken one rule of a professional. Now there was no doubt that his delusion was tied to "unfaithful" women and some sort of unhealthy feelings toward men. He had never approached Ruth or me physically, which in itself was significant. He hid from young men but sacrificed money and time on old men. He might be an alcoholic. His sister had once suggested that he had "mental trouble," which she intimated was along the lines of retardation.

My pride was too strong and my will overfirm. Together they forced me to find out more about this man, Snow. No one knew what was going on underneath. My elderly parents accepted him with pleasure; Ruth found it more interesting to have him on the farm, sharing the care of the horses. It turned out that he had ridden, so that, with added horses at hand, we all rode together on weekends. I had to succeed in my endeavor.

The Chaos Before the Creation

In my kit of trade, I had any and all types of tests. After that latest encounter, I would select one and, in the evenings, make a game out of it. One was on mechanical devices, answered from pictures with such choices as: Which room has more of an echo? Which gear will make the most turns in a minute? Which man can lift more weight? Which horse will be harder to hold? If a man lifts a stone with this crowbar, at which point would the bar be most likely to break? Which wire carries more current? With which arrangement can a man lift the heavier weight? There were fulcrums, illusions, and the like, from simple to advanced on the one test—wind direction, electric resistance, and other diversified subjects. He answered all but one correctly! Snow's obvious success on the mechanical motion test had puffed him up considerably.

I tried a short-form intelligence test that showed him to be average in ability. I had to get into the psychological tests, and for this I brought out my set of inkblot prints: the Rorschach test. It took a number of evenings to write down all his responses. They were unusual, to put it mildly, but not as limited in kind as I would have expected before I began. I took the results to the Harvard Psychological Study Group, but my earlier teacher there was ill and on leave of absence. But I had a friend who was interpreting these tests at a state hospital, and I took my notes to her. I gave her only three bits of information: male, aged forty-five, and my name. She didn't get the work back for some weeks, but it was worth the wait.

AUTHORIZED INTERPRETATION
of
RORSCHACH PSYCHODIAGNOSTICS

Subject is intelligent, inclined to be compulsive and use his energy in attending to unimportant details as an escape for facing the more ordinary commonplace issues. Adapts fairly well to people on the surface, but will fly off the handle on occasion, and has some immaturity of thinking. Preoccupation with sex and some feelings of inferiority are sublimated by (1) appreciation of beauty in nature, and (2) by above mentioned compulsive attention to details. Shows some sign of possible over-strict bringing up in childhood. Some indications of a paranoid trend, although patient is well oriented to reality.

Now Snow was riding higher in his own estimation due to the mechanical motion test. The purpose behind the list of questions on

Snow

the intelligence test had been a mystery that he never asked about again. He had never thought he was less bright than anyone else, only that he'd had no education to help him along. I suggested a home course in high school subjects and what it would mean to him to have a diploma to hang in his room. We wrote to the superintendent of schools in Waltham, but although he had never failed a subject, he had left before the end of the eighth grade and so many credits were incompleted. This was more than he could tackle, so I dropped the idea. He didn't read at all; he said it made his head ache. We had his eyes tested, and he was indeed farsighted. With glasses, he read with pleasure articles in *Reader's Digest,* books about the sea and training saddle horses, and government bulletins on dairying. He didn't care for fiction at all. His conversation became more interesting, and his desire to remain, when strangers were at the house, seemed to expand in time. He *never* turned to alcohol again. He was more in touch with current affairs taking place in the present. Less often he would say, "Well, down Maine we always thought this was the way to do it." He had lived really almost entirely on the mores of his primitive life with grammy on the hill overlooking the fisherman's life at Boothbay Harbor.

The Chaos Before the Creation

16

Ruth

THERE WERE subtle personal changes taking place at Well-House Farm. Ruth had told me, on a drive to the office, that if she had ever married she'd have wanted a brilliant, college intellectual as a husband. She hinted that she had given up looking. Her two years in Sudbury had meant everything to her; she told me that all that mattered was Free, her aged saddlebred gelding. Actually, she worked to earn his living, bought the highest-quality grain, had him shod, and had a veterinarian check his every lump or limp. She didn't trust anyone completely, so she checked him every night before going to bed and kissed his velvety nose. On weekends she cleaned out his stall, filling it with all-new bedding. She would brush him and pet him all day on Saturdays. She exercised him by taking medium-short rides. She sniffed each forkful of hay she gave him to make sure it was sweet and full of clover. People teased her about him, but her interest seemed healthy enough to them. He was to her what a pet dog is to anyone else. It gave purpose to life and something to plan for and support. She said, "I never have been so contented; living with you has given me my greatest joy, and having the chance to be on this beautiful farm, a room of my own, the job you provided for me, and a place to have Free with me all the time; life is full and I'll never change it now."

It suddenly washed over me that Ruth had been too easily bent by my influence. She had a crush on me. I was her loving friend and her

gelding was her sexual interest. With Cliff, unwanted by his mother
and a stepfather, who couldn't stand the sight of him, we indeed
made a flock of sick birds roosting together!

By January 1949 I had resigned my position as executive secretary
in Newton. I required full-time to pursue Snow's needs. Ruth used the
old car for commuting. She seemed just as happy but was spending
more and more time with her horse. By spring I overheard her calling
the grain store and adding six bales of hay to her order. When I asked
her why, when the loft was still half full of good hay, she retorted,
"There isn't anything left good enough for my horse, and the pastures
aren't up enough to give him what he needs."

The following weekend she and I spoke about her current situation
and her life ahead. She realized that she was trapped by the congenial-
ity of life in Sudbury, and she insisted she wanted to stay right there. I
suggested that she talk to some psychiatrist and try to understand the
need for broadening her life. She accepted that idea and put action
into it. She never told me anything further, but I could see she was
beginning to have more and more doubts about her complacent life in
the country. She spoke of Free as old—he was by now more than
twenty—and of having him put to sleep. She kissed him more often
and became shorter with us. She was fighting a personal battle and I
thought she'd win with a push at this point. I wrote her a long letter
one Friday night and left it for her to read after her late sleep on
Saturday morning. It made the suggestion that she send the horse
back to her father's farm in Peabody, so she could take a room nearer
her job; that she join some country dance group and spend her
evenings with people her own age. She was ten years younger than I.
Vegetating in Sudbury was easy and joyful, but I was sure more vital
things lay ahead for her.

Snow, Cliff, and I left early, after the cows were at pasture, and
stayed away all day. On Sunday we could see she had been crying, but
she stated simply that she had called her sister to come for Free and
that she had applied at the Franklin Square House in Boston for a
room. It certainly seemed that I had correctly guessed what her
psychiatrist had been urging her to consider. Much came to pass. She
met a big, bright man who earned his pay in a piano factory and spent
his years supporting his mother. He was musical. When they weren't
square dancing they were using a piano in an alcove at the Franklin
Square House. She learned to play a recorder, and he accompanied
her and sang. Her long, hot summer ended in an offbeat wedding in

Ruth

the fall. Snow and I were the only guests present who were not immediate family. They wrote their own ceremony and had it tape-recorded. The wedding reception was an enormous square dance held in a country hall. She had created her own gown as a white dancing dress with little black kid slippers; her sister wore the same, in color, as maid of honor. Each wore appropriate satin streamers flying from her topknot!

After his mother's death, they bought a rickety brick house on Beacon Hill and formed a Mozart chamber music group. Ruth made her husband lose eighty pounds and attend Northeastern University night school until he graduated into electronics. I introduced him to the faculty music group at Harvard College where his interest in old instruments burgeoned. He became official restorer of Harvard's antique collection. They had only one son, who almost cost Ruth her life. He was large and long, and she was bearing down toward forty years. Her husband was tremendously gifted; Northeastern wanted him to remain and teach. He had received his graduate degree on completing a fellowship, and therefore he remained until the right opening appeared. After two moves up, he was in a high-bracket position in Cambridge. His son attended Browne and Nichols School while his parents became well known in circles devoted to classical music. They sent to England for a harpsichord, and Ruth studied the bassoon and other instruments.

Years later she whispered to me that her doctor had sent her a telegram after her marriage, reading, "Isn't a man better than a horse?" So I had been right all along! We don't see them at all anymore. They are on their own.

17

Brains and Brawn

AFTER RUTH left Well-House Farm, Snow and I were alone with only Clifford as visible chaperon. I was his legal guardian, so thank goodness no one started the slightest gossip about our household.

Now it was time to get a definite prognosis on Snow's mental condition—as conclusive as one could ever define in this type of aberration. My friend at the state hospital wrote me that a psychiatrist from there was in Harvard Square on Wednesdays. I made a series of appointments, but was up against a wall of protest trying to persuade Snow to move in that direction. He was adamant. Of course his stubbornness was rooted in his knowledge that someone might find out even more details of his behavior than even I had solicited. His devotion for his early friend, Fred Munster, was still very much alive in his conversation. My father had become idolized by him, but women were still sexual cheats, and boys and younger men were still anathema. I begged, explained, forced the issue, and finally took him to Cambridge.

This was the prescribed way to handle such a delicately balanced, make-or-break critical state of affairs in the emotions and mind at this point in Snow's life. He could not be humored; he could not be forced to face the possibility that he was mentally ill, especially by me—a friend and protector. Argument brought on only suspicion; he would never have been cajoled into seeing a doctor for a pain, a cut that might need stitches, or any acute digestive or intestinal symptoms. He'd rather die than be seen by any doctor. "In fact," he often said, "that will be the time I'll see a doctor, while I'm dying." This I had always interpreted as his reactions linked to the deaths of his mother and grandmother: it was his belief that no doctor had tended them in health, only in death. Thus, linking a superficial disease to a visit to this specialized doctor was worse than worthless. It drove him from the room.

Over a period of almost three years, I had developed some understanding by exploring neutral subjects and piecing together a story through incidents that took place during his childhood and young manhood. He could be drawn into an exposure of his emotionally charged beliefs by having them included in some long account of what he thought was a fine story at someone else's expense. There were many factors in his general state of mind that I could take as being real to him. Thankfully, there were many of these; and there were many more serious conditions I could discard. The general picture brightened. When he was talking about himself, I could overact in enthusiasm and often successfully urge him to add bits. "Tell me some more about what *you* did when you drank beer with the boys. Why did your Grammy like *you* better than her sons or other grandchildren?" There are many innocent-sounding questions that can be asked in such situations, always keeping in mind that actually your companion is truly most interested in the world with himself as its core. This is the fact with its accompanying handicaps. Whatever question you put, or any phrase you use, such as "And then . . . ?" "So they . . . ?" must always leave a way for your friend to back out gracefully without your showing any sign of closing up or shutting off the forward roll of the conversation. His complete breakdown came when his encircling world was torn off, leaving him bare. Our efforts in Sudbury had been to build substance around him and enlarge his safety zone. That had been step number one—but was hardly a cure; a preventive measure against death, but no permanent step in his future climb.

In my relationship with Snow, there was no way to use sentiment, promises, or love's entreaties; for prescription there was a chance to use affectionate terms, a flattering interest, and that insidious phrasing; "Look at all I've done for you—the least you could do would be to try one visit and then turn me down." But, as I have explained, I finally took Snow to Cambridge following many parts of wholes of these collective persuasions.

Snow

In my private interview with the doctor, I outlined, in general, the problems as I had seen them. His first hour with Snow was fruitless. Each successive week things did improve, and some sort of rapport developed between them. But Snow boasted, on each return trip, about what he had not told the psychiatrist rather than about what he had divulged. However, I was able to keep up the visits for at least two months, for I had to know from the doctor what his report would be in regard to Snow's future behavior. Could we break the cycle? Could we lift the delusions? Or was his mental illness permanent?

Now we could spend our days driving to New Hampshire. We looked in the Boston papers under "Farms for Sale" and made arrangements with brokers to show us places from the Vermont border to the seacoast. We drove to Maine for outings, but Snow was not drawn to that state, as I thought he might well be. We often took my parents and Cliff to visit some likely farm, but the former pair would turn down anything that wasn't near them in Temple, New Hampshire. We often had Sunday dinner there and even loaned my father one of our Tennessee Walking Horses, since his last gray had been laid away. Father had ridden to hounds all over the East and South and didn't stay out of a saddle until he was eighty.

Agents thought of me as an eccentric lady with a married daughter who was a veterinarian, and of Snow as the hired hand. We spoke of raising horses and dogs, and no one in New Hampshire, certainly, gave us a second glance. In essence, this was the actual state of affairs, but no one, not even my parents, knew about Snow's psychiatric reeducation.

During one of our last trips to Harvard Square, I talked with the doctor alone. He had found Snow unresponsive, but he liked him and thought, because of the slow buildup of his neurosis, it could be reversed before it developed into a fixed state. I asked for his suggestions for handling Snow's future. He said only a projected, unswerving, subtle relationship with someone could help him.

I knew Snow had been tactfully asked whether he had ever slept with Ruth or me; also, whether he had made friends with boys when he was a younger man. The questions annoyed Snow so much that he had told me about them. Knowing what the psychiatrist was after, I realized Snow had absorbed no knowledge of paranoid and homosexual traits. He had married three times and had one daughter. Apparently, there had been no overt action with men even in disguised form. However, I had seen or heard of times when he had become infatuated with, or magnetized by, individuals of either sex.

Brains and Brawn

These might last a few months and always ended in hate. This was conspicuous ambivalence to the informed.

For our final consultation, Snow and I held a joint meeting with the doctor. In answer to the doctor's question as to what he hoped to do next and what in his heart would give him peace and happiness, in a matter-of-fact voice Snow explained, "I guess . . . when we find a farm, far away from Sudbury, Miss June and I will marry. I believe two people should like to do the same things and do them together."

The psychiatrist turned to me and asked, "Is this your plan?"

I didn't know what to say. I suppose I looked fussed, even blushing; the thought had never entered my mind before! Here, in the dark, tiny room over a store near Harvard's gates, I was receiving a proposal. "If Snow's faith can be restored and a normal life lies ahead, perhaps I might consider that denouement." The doctor questioned Snow about whether he would ever doubt his Miss June. Snow had to admit, in honesty, that he really couldn't be sure. There things stood for a while.

The doctor wrote me a diagnostic and final letter assuring me that Snow was *not psychotic*. If he lived a few years within a secure circle, he could slip back into a normal man's conduct in actions and reactions.

Should I undertake Snow's vindication? I might swing myself into oblivion and disrepute—or I might save another's living character. Did I give myself a choice? No!

We were never engaged, as such, but we kept on hunting for the right places "up-country." One evening while I was clearing away the supper things, Snow came in quite disquieted. He told me he would have to pack up and leave; he'd find some sort of job and support himself again. He gave no reason then but asked me out for dinner that next evening. I thought it best to accept. Fresh surroundings might help him to talk openly. We fed Cliff and left him doing his homework.

We drove about ten miles to a candlelit place with booths. Here he told me, "I cannot keep living in the same house with you because it keeps me awake wanting you with me."

"Oh, Snow, please don't speak those things out loud. I've had a long, difficult time living alone and really don't dare to change things right now. Please, please leave everything as it was—at least for now. Saying these things will make it difficult to live under the same roof with you, and I won't have you go off on your own right now. Turn

Snow

back to what it was yesterday and let us hold off any decisions for the present."

I was heartbroken. Being exceedingly affectionate, having my emotions bared after all these years was most disturbing for me. If another marriage did not work out for me, I would break down and Snow would lose all he had gained. We could end in destroying each other.

"Take time, postpone such ideas, control your feelings a little longer, please." I begged for these things over and over again. "Try to keep everything as it now stands. We'll dream of a great farm in New Hampshire and get pamphlets on raising purebred cattle and do a little studying in scientific agriculture."

When we reached home, he managed to kiss me on the brow. He did go on as before, and there was certainly a tacit consent between us that if everything seemed to be coming out right for us as the months passed, we might plan to share our old age together. He entered into the scheme, and we sent away for bulletins and drew plans for stalls and studied the newest farm machinery.

In early May we found a little old house, pretty much fallen apart, along the Souhegan River Valley in Amherst, New Hampshire. The barn had blown down in the hurricane of 1938. There was no electricity, no water in the last of three wells, and no floor in the ell. The basement walls were tumbling in and the backhouse had no roof. It was as early as any house in that inland area of the state. It had been built as a land grant farm on part of what was then Massachusetts. Nothing grew on its fields but sorrel and moss—oh, and hardhack! When my father, a retired investment banker, saw it, he said, "Not an asset, only liabilities!" However, it lay just off his route between Temple and Cambridge, where he kept an apartment for the winter months, so he thought it would be wonderful if we had the courage to start on such a project. The price was eight thousand dollars, including about one hundred acres. Father told us that if we could get it reduced to five thousand dollars he'd give it to us as a wedding present. It was obvious that he and Mother would not settle for less than this state of social position. They both loved Snow, and Father, at least, enjoyed him thoroughly. Mother's earliest reaction to the change of name from Meader to Holloway was, "I just knew it! He has served time in jail!" I laughed that one off, but it had been a personal jail at that! My parents never learned anything other than his early disappointments, his being "orphaned" so many times, and had not

Brains and Brawn

heard his unending stories about the horse-and-buggy days.

We signed the real estate agreement with the agent in our car. The car sat on the grass in front of a sunken, granite stone step. There were enormous, handsome trees, but not a flower or shrub was left around the house. Piles of granite lay about that had been foundations of original outbuildings. The house was at a tilt because a giant root of an hourglass elm had been allowed to grow under the main house and raise it off its foundation. The doors and windows were jammed shut. The bulkhead was a bare flight of granite steps to the cellar. Some poles held up part of a back wing. Hurrah for the untouched central chimney, the fireplaces up and down, the brick oven, the wooden sink, old Suffolk latches and strap hinges. What an unspoiled jewel we had stumbled upon! "Mr. Agent," I excitedly thanked him, "you have now set our wedding date!"

"But, but—I thought you wanted to run a dairy farm and have this man work for you."

"No, indeed. We are going to give life a new chance for us. Let's see, we'll call ourselves 'The '49ers.' "

We set May 27 as our wedding date. We wanted the Unitarian minister of Milford to join us at his church, for the so-called May Meetings would be over by that time. We decided Clifford would stand beside his uncle and I would bring one old friend who had seen me through much travail. We asked for no words of the wedding service, just words of spring, of beginnings, of hope, of triumph over trials—words for us to live by as the grandparents that we were. In other terms, all we wanted was the presence of Nature and a chance to have some late, happy, busy years.

On our return trip to Sudbury, after Father's offer, we stopped for some time in a dark field and had all those kisses we had forgone for such a long time. The die certainly had been cast. How long would it take before I became that one person Snow would have faith enough and trust in so that his evil delusions wouldn't break his infinite love—and mine—this time?

I gave my first love laughter,
I gave my second tears,
I gave my third love silence
Through all the years.

My first love gave me singing,
My second eyes to see,
But oh, it was my third love
Who gave my soul to me.

"Gifts"
Sara Teasdale

Brains and Brawn

18

Ponemah

THREE WEEKS can seem long, but the twenty-one days coming next were the fullest ever used by anyone that we had ever read about. We returned to Well-House Farm to list it for sale. That money would build the cowbarn in Ponemah. This is the Indian name for the southeast corner of Amherst. There is a hill by that same name atop of which, during the 1890s an inn stood. A pair of horses pushed the hotel stage from the original railroad station for that area up what is now just a narrow lane leading to its cellar hole. One of the Janus waiting room benches still stands under a thick maple at Holloway Farm. It was made with narrow slats, and it had been easy to replace them one by one to keep the seat in usable condition.

We painted the front door of the Sudbury place, dusted the house, and let the agents show the historic spot. It was a beautiful time of year. Snow and Cliff kept the cows milked and the barn clean. The horses had been dispersed. Our plan was to fence in the whole river side of the new Holloway Farm so that we could take our calves and dry cows up, as soon as the weather permitted, and leave them there. We drove the route each day in a pickup truck brimming full.

By the greatest of good fortune we discovered a carpenter who would take on the job of restoring the dying house. His greatest assets were a knowledge of, and interest in, old houses, and his ability to find the right helpers and to carry out suggestions. He would build the barn when the time came for that. I had drawn out the plans on a large sheet of graph paper, marking every detail in line and figure. This barn was forty by eighty feet with a side milkroom twelve feet square. The cows were at ground level, and the gambrel roof was built without uprights. One massive hayloft had windows at each end, two metal cupolas on the ridge, an automatic ventilator rising from above the cows, and two sets of double doors at each end as well as two smaller ones in the peaks for the large pipes we'd use for blowing chopped hay into the mow. A large room was created over the milk-room with a window in its dormer end. In the lingo, the huge gambrel roof on the barn and ell were held up by knees and elbows! The hemlock flooring had been purchased from a mountain-cutting in Deering, New Hampshire. It had been drying on sticks for a year and was going begging in the market. It was strong and slippery and served us well. Many a barn dance was held in that loft!

The little house was our first concern, for it had to be made livable. I drew scale plans and then became inventive. In the meantime, the house was raised off its foundation, the granite stones laid up again where needed, the root blasted out, cellar windows cut into the stone, and finally the building gently lowered. A mason checked the four fireplaces and their flues and put a "blanket" over the bricks back of the woodwork and paneling. We literally brushed up box after box of hickory-nut shells that had flowed out into all the rooms surrounding the chimney. We discovered that there had once been a fire in the wall between the kitchen fireplace and the oven. Once the house was dismantled to this point, we could trace its entire history. Suffice it here to explain that the original room, chimney, "porch" and oven room met the requirements for the granting of land for homesteading: a permanent building 18 by 18 feet with land cleared for garden and cattle followed by a deed to the colonist of 160 acres. The facts on this completion and acceptance of our farm were written out in longhand in a large volume stored in the Archives of the New Hampshire Historical Society in the state's capital.

We easily located the 18 by 18 foot space and noted the addition of the large room (this house was only one room deep) on the opposite side of the 12 by 12 foot based chimney. The narrow addition at the other end contained a second pantry, two closets, and a bornin' room. Very shortly thereafter, a low-ceilinged back entry was added to make room for a staircase to the upper east room, and beneath this a flight to the cellar was installed. The front stairs arose from the porch, or what

Jersey and Ayrshire calves feeding during the period when the dry stock was fenced in at the Holloway Farm in Amherst.

we now call a front hall. It originally was an inside entry, and since it was never heated it was called a porch. Heat for each room was provided, of course, by the series of fireplaces. The chimney in this individual house was so large that for the two rooms under the slanting roof, two sets of stairs were needed! Later, the back entry was lengthened to form an ell or large family-use room. This itself was lower in elevation and had been made even more useful by further lengthening its northern section, divided between a third pantry and a small bedroom A single flue chimney was later added for the pro-verbial black stove. There was a second wooden sink, with a lead pipe running from the pump-at-sink to the well under this ell. Disposal was simple. Both sinks had pipes and troughs running through the outside walls to the open ground! The privy was properly placed outside the ell at the edge of the glacial period riverbank, but a

Snow

covered woodshed did give some protection during access and egress. This had been a three-holer, a family affair. The rooftree was just that, the gunstock corner posts were indeed tree trunks placed sky-tops down. The summer beams and supports were covered and chamfered, as was done by even our farming ancestors. Open beams were left in woodsheds and carriage sheds, not in their living quarters. This house had no carving, no dentils, no fancy trim or pilasters. Each room was horizontally covered by wide pine boards, and there was wainscotting up to the windows, with plaster, bound together with cowhairs, from there to the ceiling. A narrow chair rail and inconspicuous beading were used to edge the boards. Cupboard doors were plain or had a single raised panel. The stair rail was simple, but the newel was a piece of heartwood, which, when the paint was removed, showed the loveliest of shadings and seemed to demand a caress. A row of handmade hooks were driven into the trim where many an outside jacket had been hung.

We tucked in two baths, a hot-air heating system, a galley into the last-mentioned pantry; painted the walls white, as found whitewashed under eight layers of paper, and took all the woodwork down to its natural time-colored rich brown. Shelves, high and low, built-in benches, mantle trim—everything went back to its first beginnings. The bornin' room we lined with bookshelves, even over the doors, to hold our library. Curtains were hung inside the frames and drawn across the glass at night. The rooms were filled with our ancient family collection of jugs, ironware, lamps, pine furniture, and woodenware: firkin, noggin, tankard; also chests, hooked rugs, lanterns, cast-iron shelf brackets in the galley, pictures, mirrors, and prints; a hooked stair runner made from a hundred-year-old rug we bought in Essex; church benches, horse weights for doorstops, hanging bookshelves, churns, trivets, forge- and anvil-made utensils —cooking spoons and forks; true barn lanterns outside, carriage lamps inside the sheds, and crowning all these, and more, my collection of American pewter. It was like living in a museum to everyone but us. Snow and I could be informal, skip housework, and polish nothing. We sat by our fireplace each evening with two farm collies at our feet with never a door locked, as there were no keyholes from the outside of the old doors. We did have one indulgence, though—we bolted our bedroom door from the inside each night! We would hate to wake up to find a stranger standing on the rug. Snow never hesitated to investigate any noise from the barn; he would take his flashlight and tour the farm at four in the morning, but I didn't share that freedom. The electrician had put in floodlights around the house and barn with switches placed where I could snap on the artificial daylight to drive away the curious, whatever form—fox, skunk, muskrat, dog, or man. Sometimes it would turn out to be a heifer or a colt that had wormed its way out of a paddock or jumped a fence. Deer hunters were helpful to the cows. They would just bring clippers and cut a man-sized hole through the woven wire!

Over the years we rebuilt the connecting sheds and ells where we found the granite foundations buried under the turf. In this way, we added an outside covered entrance, storage space, two carports, a four-horse stable, and an implement shed over a stone floor once used for a piggery.

As a fillip, we added a low saltbox ell, large enough for a hall to display our model boat collection, an enormous bedroom with a picture window facing the river and mountains, a screened porch for warm evenings, a walk-in closet, and a departmentalized bathroom, with its own open porch outside containing an extra shower for hot and cold water. Whether after haying or on a hot day or under the moon, this was always an unusual experience. A steamy shower under the sky, with shy birds as audience, was rather sensuous for Pilgrim descendants! The small pond below it held ducks and white China geese; in the spring two huge snapping turtles mated there, and a pair of bitterns stood like stumps waiting their daily feed of frog. Blue herrons stomped up the river, beyond the pasture, like men in rubber boots.

There is much to be filled in here. So we must go back to Well-House Farm, and Clifford's mother, Angelia Isobel May Meader Hansen Wheeler. Cliff had done well in school, learned to be helpful at our house, ridden horses, and had become a gentleman with guests and with us at mealtimes. His Scandinavian background sent him along with blond hair and tall stature. He and Unc did the evening chores together. One late afternoon Snow came in alone for supper. He thought Cliff would be in later, but "later" came and was extended. We went out to look around the linter. Things seemed in order, but Snow did admit there had been a joking episode that had gone too far. Each one had teased the other until the exchange got out of control. Cliff took offense, picked up that metal stool, and threw it at close range straight at his uncle. A steel leg had struck Snow near the groin, but luckily it had only knicked the flesh on his thigh. Cliff stayed out all night. It had happened before in his younger days, Snow explained. He wasn't at all disturbed. However, I didn't know enough about the boy to guess what he might do—and I could be held responsible. He might hitch a ride to Natick; or he might walk to a Hansen aunt who lived near the Framingham border, or, as Snow was sure, he would get hungry and just walk into the house sometime without an explanation. I thought of notifying the local or state police, but the weather was warm and Cliff enjoyed sleeping out. Perhaps he would sneak into the hayloft later in the night. Snow had been right.

All three of us had chosen our rooms and planned our activities at Ponemah. Cliff was looking forward to getting away from Massachusetts—or seemed to be. What I did not know was that some of the Hansen cousins attended the South Sudbury central school. News was traveling via this link between us and Annie Wheeler. Cliff's mother, realizing how he had grown and how useful he would be at home, now that he was high school age, instigated some schemes to break the guardianship. She was a convincing liar and added a screaming voice. She could create a case in her imagination. When she learned that her brother would marry again, she telephoned to him and raised a nasty storm. I could hear her across the room! Her warning and intense rebukes were against his marrying a college woman! She suggested all kinds of trouble that would come out of such a union. She wanted Clifford back at once or she'd take "that woman" to court. Never had I heard Snow speak with such authority and intelligence, without emotion or head-hanging. "Now, Annie, listen to me. Keep out of my business. Miss June is a fine lady, and I won't have anyone hurting her or upsetting our life at this point. Never call me again. Just keep out of my life. You have been the basic cause of many of my troubles. You have never helped me when I needed it, while I have done much for you during your depressed years. Don't butt in here. Never use such language to me. Keep away." He was white and drawn-looking, but he had taken a stand on his own; there had been no "I guess" or "I'll see" or "Now, Annie, don't bother me." He was on his own feet.

Before school closed she went to the probation officer in Natick and told enough stories and lies to get him to ask me to drive over for a conference with him. He was a graduate social worker, too, and far superior to those in most juvenile courts. I welcomed a chance to talk with him, but as I approached the brick courthouse I could hear

Annie's voice, even from a second-floor window, castigating her brother and using such words as "bitch," "dummy," "bad man," and parts of sentences telling some wild bits of old stories about Snow or his past friends; there were also some slurring remarks about that "college woman." I found myself being guided toward that room by the officer in charge, but I shook my head and said, "I have no intention of joining that group." The probation officer came out and took me down to the judge's chambers.

"I don't blame you," he said, "and I will join you in your decision not to face such people. What do you want us to do? As guardian, it is up to you." It was warm outside, a lovely early June day. I wore dark blue, with white gloves and pocketbook, with a smile of pity for the poor woman still carrying on her ugly story at top voice down the hall.

I told the probation officer: "Although I have spent much attention, affection, and money on Clifford Hansen, I never would have undertaken to educate him and see him through his twenty-first year if I had known he had undisclosed relatives in the lower part of Sudbury. This connection undermined all I was trying to do. Through them he was receiving directions from his mother. Such a woman"—indicating the direction from which we could hear her tirading voice—"has no place in my life. I was never told Cliff had been on probation or that she had reported him as an unruly child. My decision can be quickly made. Her brother, Snow, is a very fine person. Her jealousy has been a disease with her, which has become an obsession, and it would destroy any chance Clifford would have with us. I'll send him and all his new possessions back here to Natick the day after school closes."

He stood up and saluted me as an equal and complimented me for my understanding and for my solution. "Let them make their own mistakes. Each one of her children has been on probation at one time or another. Her oldest daughter, still a minor, married a known auto thief, who is now in prison. Mrs. Wheeler has made her worst judgment in spoiling her only son's best opportunity by forcing an issue to get him back at this point in his life. I, too, didn't know she had relatives in Sudbury which would have tripped us up."

As we walked back to the top of the stairs, we could hear part of the continuing story of Snow's marriages and how crazy he was anyway. We two social workers shook hands and gave one another a look of professional sympathy.

Some years later Annie brought some friends to Amherst to check on our lives there. She was overdressed, with earrings and high heels.

Snow

We happened to be running the noisy blower that sent the chopped hay up into the hayloft. We were most cordial, of course; we stopped work long enough to offer iced tea and show them about the inside of our home. She must have been surprised at our way of life. She told Snow she came to check to see if he was getting along all right or needed help. She refused the tea and gathered her friends together on the excuse that they were sightseeing through parts of New Hampshire and couldn't stay but a minute. We have never seen her since that day, nor have we seen any of the children since the day Cliff returned home to continue his probation. He became a well-paid carpenter with a decent wife and children and lived in a comfortable home. His short time with us must have given him some incentives and values.

19

A Way of Life Together

THE WEDDING DAY was rainy. My daughter and her husband were to stay at Well-House Farm to watch over the routine. Cliff was to milk the cows and drive them out. The twenty-ninth, thirtieth, and thirty-first of May formed a holiday weekend, so our absence would cause no complications for our stand-ins. We drove up to Milford in separate cars and went hand in hand down the aisle. We had a late tea in Temple where we were met by my daughter. She took Clifford back to Sudbury after we had started out in the pouring rain for Maine. It was dark when we reached the new turnpike where we had to backtrack in order to pass under it. We were headed for the Danish Village, south of Portland, for our first night. This can be a colorful spot. Each one-room, semidetached, miniature house is of different hue and of different shape and angles. It predates the motel as we know it. But each unit had its bath and garden plot. A central building was a restaurant and office, but on this night it had not opened for the season. The tiny peaked houses were busy, though! We were refused entrance on the excuse that the whole group was reserved for Massachusetts junior team members, and their masters, who were playing a round robin at the Portland stadium the following day. We explained our situation, mentioned the lateness of the hour and the long day behind us, and begged them to go over the list to make sure all the rooms were occupied. One was not being used. Ha! We drove around the winding lanes until we found its number. The building was made entirely of cement, and no heat was provided in those days. We left our bags and drove up Route 1 to a small restaurant. After a bowl of hot soup and dessert, we returned. It was almost ten o'clock. Not a youngster had quieted down. Their masters were hopelessly going from door to door trying to get them into bed. We crawled between our damp sheets and lay awake most of the night. By five in the morning the boys were up and out, calling back and forth, visiting each other in groups. Not a honeymoon night. Well, it might be at our next stop?

We were back at the same restaurant by six-thirty in the morning with our packed bags in the car. We ate scrambled eggs and bacon, toast and marmalade, and drank coffee and tea to assuage our hunger and thirst. We had written ahead to Mrs. Merriman in Topsham, the kindly town clerk who had helped us to establish Snow's birth and write out the certificate in longhand. She had explained where she lived. "Just cross the river at Brunswick and you'll see the sign on a white house to your right. I'm looking forward to meeting you two after your romantic insistence on setting the record straight. I'll be right here anytime on May twenty-eighth." We thought her handwriting was shaky, but we knew she had held her position for three generations, so she must be a dear, white-haired little lady.

Route 1 took us into Brunswick, and the very first thing we did was turn left over the river just below the falls. We could see the house where Snowie had been born just at the water's swiftest point. He recounted the time, as a toddler, he had ventured toward the noise and splashing. His mother had often told him she had reached him just in time to grab him by his britches and yank him backward. It was a lesson to both of them.

I kept my eyes on each white house as we passed along the road. Sure enough, here was the tiny sign: "Town Clerk." After a peek into my pocket mirror, I joined Snow as we rather self-consciously walked up her path. A note pinned to the door read, "See Mrs. ——— for any Town Clerk or Treasurer business, second road above on right." We were disappointed, for we had looked forward some years to this moment, our call on the gracious, cordial Mrs. Merriman in her old-fashioned rooms. Back in the car we found ourselves on a new unfinished road with rows of new ranches. One had a paper tacked up at an angle as if it were meant to be temporary. A busy young mother answered our knock. She was in her housecoat with a child clutching her skirt. "I don't know anything about an appointment with Mrs.

A Way of Life Together

Merriman. No mail was opened as far as I know. She died last week and the funeral was yesterday. I am helping out the town by filling out dog licenses and the like." We just couldn't believe what had happened in a week's time. The girl showed no interest in us and must have been thankful that we apologized and left so quickly. Our Mrs. Merriman had been in her eighties. She had so looked forward to this reunion in person, but just couldn't hang on after another cold winter. Why do so many make it to April and May and then give in? The winter haul is exhausting.

We needed a cool drink, so we sat at the counter in Snow's favorite drugstore in Brunswick. Bowdoin College was still in session, and a few boys were about even though it was a holiday. This gave us time to reflect on Mr. Wright's clinging to life. He was the fourth generation that had owned the Ponemah farm. Before him had been the original grantees, and after him ourselves. Three owners' names! He signed the deed from his hospital bed at three in the afternoon about May 12. The agent registered this deed in the Hillsborough County Court House and delivered our copy on his return home. We had planned to call on the elderly gentleman, of ninety, the following day to tell him how much we cared for his old homestead. But after asking whether the new owners would keep cows, he smiled and closed his eyes. He wasn't there for breakfast.

After leaving the Brunswick area, we left all recent past and present restoration plans behind us. Old Route 1 kept us from actually seeing the ocean, but we crossed all the wide rivers that empty into the tidal inlets. Fishing boats, lobstermen, and shore restaurants began to appear. The atmosphere sent Snow back to his early saltwater days, and he vigorously recounted the early sailing era.

We traced way back to the Hallowell fleet of Down-Easters, and then back to his grandfather, Capt. Alonzo Meader, sailing the last regular ship of this dwindling period. It had been named *The Cora Clara* for Captain Joseph Franklin Hallowell's first granddaughter and, incidentally, Snow's mother.

After our return home I found a book on Maine sailing vessels. These facts filled in the space between the early world trading days to the work about to begin on the old *Santino*. The great fore-and-afters were running to the end of their ropes. Theirs was the last chapter in the history of the wooden sailing ship and the old shipbuilding industry on the Maine coast. The fast clipper was sharp-built and

made record runs to China and overseas ports; the tall Down-Easters
carried more sail aloft to make up for their increased cargo space
below the waterline; the great schooners were the most weatherly and
economical sailing ships in the world. These were the workhorses of
the heavy trade along the east and west coasts of the United States,
heading down the coast to South America, rounding the tip, then
back up the coast to California. Much of this era was paralleled by the
projected building of the Panama Canal, but before its opening in
1914 the schooners had carried diversified cargoes of men and goods.
The first of the gold seekers to set sail from Maine took with them all
manner of household goods as well as small knocked-down houses,
medicines, and salable cargo. Lumber at $10 a thousand in Belfast
brought $300 in San Francisco. By 1910 lean days arrived for the
schooners. However, World War I brought a resurgence of their use,
and fortune to many a bankrupt owner. Actually, half a dozen six-
masted schooners were built in this period. They made runs to England, France, the Mediterranean, and Africa. By 1917 coal rates alone
had risen from 65 cents to three dollars. By the end of 1918 the lucky
owner had read the signs and sold out for what he could get.

Coasters were reincarnated, restored, or rebuilt in that warning
year of 1938. They had limited use.

In August 1979, a 97-foot, two-masted freight schooner was
launched at Thomaston, Maine. Construction had taken four years to
complete after the laying of her keel. She made a fortuitous splash as
she slid into the harbor. At the apex of the approaching fuel shortage,
she can carry six trailer-truck loads of cargo. Once again coastal sailing
with the wind will come into its own implicit value.

By mid afternoon we were at Boothbay Harbor looking for lodging.
No inns, hotels, or cabins were open for the season! We drove all over
the village. What beauty at the seashore out of season! Snow and I
have always liked it that way. Several native families had rooms for
rent, and Snow picked out an attractive one near the wharves. It was
freshly painted, and the bulbs were up around the house. The sun was
out and the lobster boats hung limp at their moorings. It was a long
Memorial Day weekend. Captain Gray and his family owned the
house, and we were shown into a large first-floor front room. The bath
was at the top of the stairs. Rice fell out of my bag as I unpacked. My
daughter had filled its side pockets and top envelope. We laughed.
That was the only token we had that made the twenty-seventh of May

any different from any other day in our lives. We washed separately and then walked along the shore road. We ate chowder at a little shop and continued across the footbridge over the inner harbor. Halfway over I made Snowie kiss me. He was embarrassed! This was the cove where he and Annie had played tiddlies on the ice cakes, and this was the bridge where he had made her pretend to cry that she had dropped her 50-cent piece through a crack. We wandered back for the car, but as we neared the house Snow recognized a man getting out of an automobile with Massachusetts plates. "Of course," he explained, "Captain Gray's son married, and he is in the upholstery business in Waltham. There he is with his wife and children coming up for the holiday." Snow changed. He walked me quickly into the house and locked us in our room. There were white glass curtains over the windows, but as it grew darker, he pulled down the shades. To use the bathroom, he waited until he thought no one would be around, then made a run up the stairs. Late in the evening we went out for food and brought back cookies and chocolate. That night was like the one at the Danish Village—no honeymoon yet. He had me up early saying we'd have to leave as soon as we possibly could, as he didn't like it there at all. He was shaking. My only conclusion was the connection with Waltham, Fiske Avenue, and his uncle's beatings. Surely he hadn't been hurt by the Grays before he left Boothbay. I learned later, years later, that Snow had a terrifying misgiving that this was the son of the man who had boxed his ears after the stone had been thrown; possibly this particular man, now grown. The coincidence of picking that house and that family couldn't have been planned. It was just plain bad luck. I'll never forget that front hall with the maritime captain's cap balanced on the hat tree! It would be a year before our return when we'd crawl up and down the wharves. He'd tell me stories of being a boy who played tricks around the floats.

We still had two days left, but I couldn't make myself believe we would be helped by staying away from home any longer. Snow was so uncomfortable, so overwhelmed by memories and mental discomfort that all desire for male and female intercourse left his body. He hardly talked to me. He drove during the day, I after sundown. His glasses were for reading only, and he seemed to have partial night blindness of sorts. Years later we learned he had an astigmatism. With glasses he now drives night or day. We turned the car inland and passed over all the famous Maine rivers upstream. We crossed the Damariscotta then the Sheepscott at crowded and narrower points. We wanted to pass into New Hampshire near Bethel so that we could enter above Mount Washington and return through Franconia Notch. The Kennebec flows fast through Waterville, Augusta, Hallowell, and Gardner where the large milltowns were founded. Generally, we see these rivers at their brackish mouths and visitors make up the population. Following Route 202, we drove southwesterly toward Androscoggin Lake, formed by the dam above Auburn and Lewiston. We tried to reconstruct the early days of these settlements where waterpower was a natural resource and the towns and citis grew up around them. Turning north, we forded the Little Androscoggin. The great river itself rises in New Hampshire from the watershed around Dixville Notch and dozens of large lakes along the state's line. The Saco River at Route 1, and now the Maine turnpike, at Biddeford and Saco is mercantile and dirty, but the river is a lovely surprise when it turns up in New Hampshire south of Mount Webster. The Pemigewasset River rises five miles north running west instead of east.

It was a clear, coolish day; the sun disappeared prematurely as we approached the first notch, but it reappeared like a western sunrise. As we turned south the sun was really setting, and we began to worry about finding a place to spend that night. Nothing was open. Tuckerman's Ravine was still buried in snow. When we broke out of the national park at Lincoln, the sun had set. The signs were identifying the cabins, but our first stop revealed the prices were ten dollars. We had never heard of such prices: preseason in 1949. At a quick-lunch counter we asked where we could find something off the traveled route. We were told to cross the next bridge, turn right, and we'd find a fellow who had some cabins up behind his house. We found an older housekeeping cottage at half price. Relaxation came at last. We had teabags and instant coffee with some Fig Newtons, so we could stay abed late and still have something with which to start another day.

After the lights were out, Snow spoke up without hesitation. "Did I tell you about the time my grandmother picked me out of the crotch of an apple tree in our backyard?"

"No, did you fall from some height?"

"A good distance. She didn't get a doctor, though. I was just a little boy, about nine. She fixed me up, but it healed crooked."

My mind was jumping along trying to guess what he meant before he discovered I hadn't followed his line. I couldn't let him lose heart and stop before he had explained a difficult admission. A little fellow falling feet first, having lost his handgrip, would be caught like a wishbone. The story was plain, honest, and simple. I knew.

"It doesn't really matter," he added, "I just didn't want you to be surprised."

Poor dear, little boy, how I loved his affliction if it was part of him.

The next morning we telephoned the farm to see how things were going. My daughter said Cliff was not very cooperative and that they were all getting tired. We said we would start right back.

Snow and I were alone with one another and a busy summer ahead. Married and inseparable. My only restriction, for myself, was never to leave Snow's sight for even a minute. We met everyone as a pair, did everything together, even short errands; held each interview standing side by side, often hand in hand.

Plans whirled in my head. With one of his short, pithy remarks Snow said, "With your brains and my bull strength and ignorance, we ought to go far."

The historical farm in North Sudbury was sold early in July 1949. The agreement called for occupancy in sixty days, so we expected to have until late summer to complete the transfer to Holloway Farm. We built a lean-to and feeders in a roadside area where an early orchard had stood. There were few of these left, for shade, and we fenced the whole area with woven wire. We filled our forty-quart jugs by backing them to the edge of the Souhegan River and filling them by the fire-bucket-brigade method.

We were sleeping at Well-House Farm and loading up there each morning. During the day we made plans with our carpenters and picked up antique hardware and lanterns as they were needed. We fed our calves and checked for any new calves dropped in the riverside pasture. One day we knew a cow had calved but had hidden the little one under the hardhack. After a few days a calf must be separated so that its parent can rejoin the milking herd. The calves were fed milk-saver through a nippled pail. "Hello, below there!" It was a workman on the ridgepole handling shingles. "You looking for that new calf? We saw it yesterday; you follow directions and we'll tell you where to look."

"Okay!" There were three of us running the paths tramped out by the cows.

"It's nearer the center—now toward the river—turn right—faster, now it's up on its feet taking off after the cow. Quick, close in between where you are and the bank here below the house." We were out of breath, but we had the calf, a husky heifer. Sometimes Snow would put one in a grainbag and carry it over his shoulder. More often it was easier to use a wheelbarrow, but this time there was only one way. The boy with us took the front end and Snow struggled with the kicking hind legs. They swung the critter between them up the dry bank, resting now and then, until they dropped it over the fence. The others stood with the inquisitive look all bovines use when something new is happening. The cow followed, but we managed to hold her off until we loaded her in the special body we could fit into our pickup truck. We drove her back to Sudbury that night. After one period of twenty-four hours, neither knew the other had ever existed. Such is the nature of the cattle family. Fed well, and in common company, they adjust immediately.

One evening when we reached Well-House Farm we found the lights on and the new family moving in! We removed our things from the bathroom and collected our thoughts. The backhouse was clean so we didn't need anything further that night. We always ate supper on the return trip. We slept in my paneled, ground-floor room, and all we asked was why they hadn't kept to our agreement.

"We gave notice to our landlady and couldn't stay beyond July first."

"Why did you do that? We are on our honeymoon and have a very complicated schedule. We don't want anyone here with us. Our hired boy comes over to milk at night and see that everything is secure."

They didn't see why we couldn't share the kitchen and bath and get along fine. "My mother wanted to visit during the summer and there was no room in our Boston apartment." She never did make any visit.

Next morning we packed a bureau with clothes, chose two chairs, a small table, a towel rack; with these we loaded our old maple bed onto our truck and headed for Sears, Roebuck in Nashua. The only tent there was ten by ten feet with no floor! It was the best we could do. It took our whole day to set up camp on top of a sharp knoll at the acute turn on the river. The view was water on three sides, with a good overseers' spot from which to keep track of the work going on at the house and barn across the lower pasture.

After driving in the last stake, which was to hold the tiny tent to the promontory covered with oak and pine trees, the bed was made up with fresh sheets, and more and warmer blankets were added. Our boy changed his milking chores to the mornings and Snow took the nights. Who would have imagined that the interlopers in our usable

Very early morning view of the Souhegan River from the tent.

home were so furious and insulted that they wouldn't speak to us! "Aren't we good enough people to share a bath?" they asked, clearly without interest in our reply. We gathered up another load of necessaries, packing the kitchen things for storage, picking up benches, lanterns, a Thermos jug, a soapdish, and so on.

We finally tucked a pair of beds under the eaves of the tiny upstairs west room of the little old house, as this needed no more work done on it for the present. We used this for storage of cartons, boxes, mirrors, pictures and filled the spaces from floor to ceiling. Each trip back at night we would drive down through the barway to the foot of our nest. We took a dip in the river, clinging to a Lilliputian island of reeds while the water flowed by and minnows nibbled our toes. We owned two dogs that slept under the bed, later expanded to five after my

Snow

daughter left her three Welsh Corgis with us for the balance of the summer. With a kerosene lantern hung on a spike outside our retreat, we were pretty snug in a ten by ten foot, "six foot at the ridge" shelter! We soon added a piece of black netting over the front flaps, as the bugs flew in by droves! The dogs learned to slip out under the edge of the tent, but when it rained we were out of dry ground space. Love bloomed in these trees. Even when we heard men walking around the foot of our hill, we knew the dogs would let us know if anyone began the climb.

We awoke the first morning to the ground shuddering in rhythm. Wrapped around each other, we tried to figure out what in the world could be so earth-shaking. The origin of the accompanying thumps seemed to come from the old house on the next level up above us. Of course—it was the machinery being used daily to drive down for an artesian well. They were below our level, at that point, and the ground was shivering. It took four hundred feet to get through the old riverbed silt before granite was struck. This took over two months, because the drilled hole refilled during each night. The workers were cementing the hole as they drove down. But when water finally came in, it was cold and clear and flowing at sixteen gallons a minute. Soon after solving the earthquakes, we heard each man in turn pick up his hammer and drive in the first nail of the day.

Looking out our only tent opening, we saw our heifers standing in the river taking long drinks of water. When they left, we followed them with our washing. I rinsed out our clothes by soaking them in a basin sunk to the sandy, shallow edge. After each sock, T-shirt, or panty was washed, I'd throw it over to the reeds, which would hold them; if one missed and floated off with the current, I'd splash in and toss it back with its mates. Then I rinsed them all with the basin in deeper water, the effluence of the stream taking the extra suds dancing along until they disappeared around the curve. I'd finish with my own dip and pull myself back up the slope. Snow had put up clotheslines and a board between two trees for a seat; also an antique horse bell tacked up by a leather strap to the largest base tree. Later, we set up a long stand with large Thermos jug of drinking water, a twenty-quart jug of washing water, soap, and toothbrush holders. Showers didn't bother us very much. Light ones didn't penetrate the oak-leaves, and the heavy rains would rinse out our towels on the line and the following sun would dry them for us. All we had to do was sleep through the sound of the rain and the smell of five wet dogs!

A Way of Life Together

My unspoken, successfully unobservable role of keeping close to Snowie was a conscious effort all summer. Sometimes it was difficult to keep it from seeming contrived; people began to say, "You two must be pretty much in love; we never see you separately." When we moved into the house I couldn't even ask Snow to get me a sweater if we had company out on the lawn. I couldn't go myself if there was a workman anywhere about the house. This became increasingly complicated as we added rooms and ells, or had electricians about, who went from cellar to bedrooms to run wires through the partitions. Sometimes they needed to have me show them an alternate spot if they ran into a carrying beam, timber, or a projecting rock. During the first years there were occasions when Snow stopped speaking to me and even slept upstairs without saying goodnight. I could see these attacks approaching. His face would develop the same hard, white streak across it, and his look would be brittle. I'd let those regressions run for an hour or so, then go up to him in the middle of the night, to talk, explain, plead, tease, and kiss him. Finally I'd make the apology that should have come from him. He'd come willingly back to our bed to hold me tight. I was always hurt and tired the next day, but I kept myself on top of the situation through pride and stubbornness. I'd have no one find us out; I would not fail. At times I could fathom his faulty conclusions; at others, there seemed to be no link to anything. Even he couldn't render help or memories. There would be no life to turn back to now; it was forward to success or to nothing for both of us.

During the nights in the tent we kept listening for those walking the river in their fishermen's boots: step, swish, push, splash; step, swish, and so on and on. We actually held our breaths sometimes to make a concentrated effort to solve this phenomenon. We could hear nighthawks, owls, whippoorwills, and bobwhites, but these rubber boots were a mystery. In the mornings we'd sit on the back side of our knoll and watch the fish in the deeper pools, see a blacksnake come out into the sun, bank swallows flying out of hundreds of holes in the sandy banks, wild ducks with a trail of ducklings. One day we heard our men approaching: two beautiful herons wading through the shallows looking for the common shiners. They seemed like tropical birds—so brilliant, so large—and they were actually unafraid of us. The adult had a maroon neck with white front, blue-green plumage, and orange legs. When stalking prey, it often assumes ridiculous poses and walks along in shallow waters. Among other birds seen that

Snow

summer were the kingfisher, partridge, quail, pheasant, chicken hawk, mourning dove, ruffed grouse, cardinal, and killdeer. Our presence scared no one but the woodchuck that lived in its tunnel under the field.

Later, when we started plowing and reseeding, we were followed by piping plovers; swallows shot past our heads to pick off the airborne bugs that rose from the grasses during mowing. Moles pushed along under the height of the cutter bar, but now and then we turned up pheasants' nests and later still the mother and her young. If we cut hay in June we watched for nests, going around them, but in July we could see the female pheasant chase her little ones into the center of the uncut field. On our last trips, down the middle, we'd have to stop the tractor and chase them off toward the brush surrounding the cut grass. On some evenings when we were out picking up hay we'd find as many as six deer grazing on the new shoots of alfalfa. They would remain where they were if we stayed in the car but leaped toward the woods if we stepped on the ground. In the fall our land was well posted with signs printed especially for us. Even so, we had too many drugstore cowboys, Sunday hunters in bedslippers, and some even shooting from their automobiles. The game warden often had time to get to us, after our call, and pick these people up for trespassing and disregarding warning signs. We had one red fox who made a trip from the woods to the river early each morning. We never saw his mate, but we did find his lair under a fallen tree at the edge of the great peat-moss bog on our east boundary. She must have stayed at home and watered in the small pools in the ancient meadow-pond.

Late in August it became too cold and damp to sleep by the river. We stacked things even tighter into that upstairs bedroom and literally crawled across into one of the twin beds! The small dogs had returned to Durham, and our farm collies slept downstairs. The doors and windows were not rehung or replaced, but the slant-topped door to this little room could be shut. It was up early for us when the workmen appeared. The barn was started, but we still had no electricity. There had to be poles set between us and the high-power lines on Route 101A, even though the newer wire could take the strain of being tightened between poles standing three hundred feet apart rather than the earlier one hundred. Excuse number one in May had been: too soon after the war to have the right materials available in quantity. Excuse number two in June: still short of men. Excuse number three in July: priorities for commercial installations. Excuse number four in

House and barn at Holloway Farm, 1949.

August: vacation time setup would delay all work. By now, the carpenters required power tools to work on the immense barn, fitting its timbers and roofing boards. They threatened to postpone the work until the power was brought in. Because all our cows were now arriving, we also needed the electricity for the milk cooler, the milking machine, and the lights. Nothing had come of writing to, or calling at, the Public Service offices. Finally, in desperation, we decided to sit it out. We stopped in early one morning and asked for the manager. He had never made himself available to us in person all these months, and this time, as usual, we were told he was out. We took two chairs and informed the secretary that, since we had the rest of the day free, we'd sit there and wait for his return. Mr. Whipple it was. We had armed ourselves with reading matter and sat cheerfully by the window. The girl made several calls, disappeared behind the scenes a few

Snow

times, and at last brought us the unexpected news that Mr. Whipple would be with us soon. Where was he? Where had he been each time we had stopped in before? We learned he had a retreat in the basement and had been there all the time! He appeared with a rather guilty look, but we gave him no quarter. We had two guns at the ready—our voices—and we let him have it squarely in his ears. Our list of inconveniences, charges, and threats drew his attention, and the poles were set and in use within a week. We had come so well prepared to spend a day with so many legitimate reasons for immediate service that Mr. Whipple could not put us off any longer. He would have become very conspicuous with us sitting all day in his window on the Milford Oval! One excuse he used was that poles in Wilton had to be moved to prepare the site for a new cutoff on the highway. That road wasn't touched until the following spring! Our use of power never ran under seventy dollars a month at the 1949 rate.

The telephone company was another holdout. It stated that without poles for it to rent, no line could be strung for us. After the poles were set, we learned that the trunklines from Nashua were overcrowded, so that we couldn't have a telephone anyway. Then the foreman laughed when I asked for a private line. Eight parties were on each wire—"but when one cancels you can have it."

"Single or nothing," I told him.

Having a cousin in the Boston hierarchy, I called him.

"You have a farm and wholesale milk business?"

"Sure we do."

He told me: "Then apply for a business telephone; I'll call our local man in Nashua and between us it can be done in a day or so." And what would you believe? We went on a priority list, and through the cousin we landed at the top of that list. For a few dollars more a month, we had our private line. What a difference! We used the Artificial Breeding Farm in Concord, New Hampshire, and had to have our call in before nine of the day their service was needed. We could now order grain, reach a veterinarian, or possibly call a doctor without driving three or four miles to a pay station.

November came in just like October. The barn wasn't completed. The cement stalls and mangers were not yet poured. Cows remain on pasture till November 15, but they don't spend the nights outside. That year, 1949, summer hung on into fall, and fall lingered into winter. Big luck was with us. One side of the milking-cow section was dry by mid-November and in went the first ten cows. Within a week they were all undercover except the heifers. Snow and I ran in all the

A Way of Life Together

waterpipes, and we set up the water bowls as well as the airpipes for the pressurized milking machine. We bought pipe cutters and a thread turner and put the whole thing in ourselves—including a sink, a water heater, and a cooler. For weeks the milk cooler had stood under a tree, and the cows had been tied up, six at a time, in a shed, the milking machine being temporarily placed on a stand. We'd drive out six and bring in six others, hoping that one of them didn't turn up for a second appearance! We fed them their grain at this time to get and hold their interest, so it was a temptation to keep in rotation!

Sometimes an occasion would arise when Snow would just have to run an errand alone. He'd order me to stay in the house and not answer the door or telephone. On his return, he'd hold an inquisition. He'd even look for strangers' tire tracks in the yard. It was a horrid ordeal. Sometimes the dairyman had backed up to the milkroom door. "Did you see him or speak to him?" I couldn't laugh because of his pain and seriousness.

We had left Waltham and Sudbury behind. Those old reminders were at least out of sight. But how would the new patterns affect him? Would the earlier subconscious reaction steal part of his joy in these newer endeavors, or would they carry over to become duplications and ruin living for both of us? Love needs trust; perhaps it *is* trust. Despite his past errors, I trusted him implicitly. What digressions may have taken place were not actually done by choice. He was searching for a way and had drifted into many unpleasant cul-de-sacs. I knew him and trusted him. What he sought in others was a strong measurement of his own inner standards. What his Grammy Meader had assured him about life was the base from which he activated his decisions and moves.

With my help we accomplished much, and we stood quite side by side facing the new world of "Snow."

20

Mr. Somebody

OUR FIRST CHRISTMAS at Holloway Farm found us settled in a unique, antique house, with one outside wall painted barnred, the granite steps back at the doorways, the hot-air heater running well, and plenty of cut logs for the fireplaces. We used the larger front room as a bedroom and the original one-room unit as our sitting room; the bornin' room, for desk and office. The large ell was our dayroom or conference-dining room. The galley was part of this ell, so that we lived in close touch during all activities. We painted the sitting room a gray-blue with cream trim, the other rooms white, with the paint removed from all woodwork. This paint removal took five years and was done mostly by the "housekeeper" in my stolen time!

The barn was arranged so that the cows faced in and the space or aisle down the center was wide and ample. This was perfect for me, as I could close up the cows' stanchions and feed them. We had a double-ended grain cart so that each cow could get her quantity and mixture according to growth and milking needs. All heifers and cow records had to be kept: names, registrations, breeding dates, calving times, as well as adherence to state and federal laws covering testing for tuberculosis and one of the Alcaligenes—brucella, causing undulant fever in man. In bovines it caused abortions. We dealt with mastitis and milk fever (postpartum diseases) and other farmers' home veterinary problems. Snow made and hung large cabinets for

Holloway Farm's appearance began to change in 1950 with more paint added by Miss June.

medications, breeding sheets, and dates. We employed "The Artificial Man," with BULL on his initialed autoplates, from the breeding farm in Concord, New Hampshire, and thus could use a fifty-thousand-dollar bull in our Jersey breeding plan for a mere six dollars a calf!

The present-day farmer is an animal husbandman, a machinist, an agriculturist, a plumber, a carpenter, a businessman, a treasurer, a wise buyer and marketman, and a Yankee trader! Farming is a life. For us it was not a case of "The man in the barn, the woman in the house." This housewife didn't make pies or can the winter's food. She worked the tractor, acted as midwife to the first-calf heifers, cleaned the tails, squeezed eye ointment into any runny eyes due to glancing off of a twig or horn scuffle under the trees. There is a boss cow in every herd

Snow

and a social order; consequently, if you add a new cow or make any change, a day in the field is used for those social rankings to be reset. Milk production will drop, although it comes right back up again. The most amazing act to watch is when the top cow is in the calving pen for a few days and a new leader tries out for an improved social position. Cows will sidestep a hooking from a boss cow when returning through the narrow lane to reenter the barn door. Two cows sometimes try crowding through at the same moment. We've seen two cows hung up right there! Once, neither would give up her place, and the door frame had to give way!

Across the river on a similar farm were newlyweds. The man was ten years younger than Snow. We saw a lot of them. They had Guernseys while we had Jerseys. We discussed feeds, fertilizers, and crops. We attended lectures together and spent some hours in conferences on our fields. We swam in the river before their first child was born. Jim was a clever, quick talker, full of double entendres. He was a studied expert on how to build up soils and when to cut, what to put in the silo mix, and what legumes to seed. Snow became fascinated by his informal and amazing chatter. I didn't realize how serious he was until we were on a day's trip to Maine and Snow left the luncheon table to buy a postal card he planned to mail to Jim. I dissuaded him, of course, but it brought a problem sharply to the front of my mind. We drifted away from them over the years because they liked their drinking, in which we never joined them. Jim became overzealous about his farm plant. He sacrificed every friendship in overemphasizing the dirty end of the barn work. Even the maternity hospital had to ask him to leave when, wearing boots covered with manure to his knees, he appeared to see his second child.

One time, when the river was low, his heifers were crossing over every night to eat in one of our pastures. Snow walked quietly down each morning, before milking, to shoo them back. One night, during that same dry spell, one of our cows, ready to calve, wandered across from our side. Jim took his heavy tractor and didn't hesitate to chase that cow down across a field and over the bank into the river. The cow lost the calf, and the cow never recovered. Later, our driving horse strayed upstream to a shallow spot and onto some rough terrain, not a pasture or planted area. Jim shouted at her and so frightened her that she lost her footing and rolled down a sandy ledge into the river. I saw and heard this and walked down with a rope to lead her home. She was an old-timer and, luckily, did not have a broken leg. All this time, Jim's fifteen young cows were still calling on us each night! I took the

Mr. Somebody

Snow in the original living room-kitchen at Holloway Farm, 1951.

Snow

lead rope down to bring her home but found her exhausted and shaking so heavily that she could not walk. I tied her to a tree and returned to get Snow for help. As I walked back up the bank from the opposite side of the barnyard, I could hear screaming and ugly exchanges of threats. I learned that Jim had ridden his high tractor up to our side door and hopped off to complain to us about the way our animals were ruining his pastures and the possibility that they were bringing disease into his herd.

During my years with Snow I had seldom heard him stand up for himself as he was now doing. He so frightened Jim, even though the latter was over six feet tall to Snow's five foot eight inches, that he jumped back onto the tractor seat—which put him at least five feet above Snow. Apparently he had just learned about his heifers, for Snow was explaining to Jim that we could have sent our two dogs down to the river to chase the sweat out of those fifteen creatures. Jim was shouting, "If any cows came over onto my fields, I'd take a gun to them!" I stepped around the corner of the house and told them about the condition of the poor horse tied down at the tree. Jim said some pretty miserable things to us, not including regrets or apologies.

Snow's idolatry turned to hate. The whole scene was ugly and proved to be the last time we ever saw Jim or his family. It spoiled a part of our lives, but it was the beginning of a deteriorating relationship within Jim's private life. After three children and many quarrels, he suddenly left town with another woman.

Snow had two other sudden cases of admiration for younger men that ended in this same rather drastic form of disenchantment. One of them I witnessed in Sudbury. A young local man, befriended by Snow, deliberately broke up some of the farm equipment without permission because he wanted to take a part from it. Snow was furious and hurt. He reacted like a man should, with justified resentment, but he had initiated the one-sided friendship. Nothing of this sort ever happens anymore. A balance has been reached since he married and formed more natural relationships. His mentor, Fred Munster, is a cripple now, and they have not seen each other in years, but Snow writes cherry, friendly letters to him. He is ever grateful for that early friendship and open opportunity to get started in his first real job. Fred, at that time, was having domestic difficulties, too, but he later moved back to Maine and took his wife and family with him.

We had built up a herd of forty-eight registered animals of our own breeding. As it expanded there was need for a barnman, someone to clean it twice a day and be responsible during our short absences. We

Mr. Somebody

were still doing all errands as a pair, and thus, in a way, not using our time to its fullest advantage. On the east side of the barn we added a snug apartment, approached from steps on the outside. Under it was a glass-bricked nursery for young stock and the calves. We found a very fine couple, Frank and his wife, who were living on their social security and needed just such a setup. She was handicapped by arthritis, and Frank had to be near enough to give her help. He could make his own hours and be within calling distance. He planted a vegetable garden, free of weeds, and we enjoyed the fruits of Frank's labor. They had seen better days, but they weren't too proud to work in such a congenial family. They introduced television into our lives and played games with us, such as Scrabble. She read a great deal and served me tea if I dropped in for an hour.

Snow always made it a habit to feed out the grain, but if we were to be away for a whole day he'd write in chalk on the manger just how much each cow was to get. Snow was funny about cleanliness, weighing the milk, and topping off the jugs. One important job he held on to was washing the milking things and disinfecting the milkroom basin and floor. Our county inspection sheet read "excellent" on every line. One summer we rated the lowest bacteria count and the highest butterfat content in New Hampshire.

Frank's wife was admitted to a hospital twice while they were there but did not survive the second trip. They had been with us a number of years and were greatly missed as friends. At one time Frank had been given a shotgun in exchange for a stove. The donor's wife learned of it and wanted the stove but also the gun. She had been that kind of employer. A sheriff turned up at the sunny barn door one morning, and when Snow learned what he wanted he stood his ground in defense of Frank. "I don't know anything about this, but Frank could never do anything wrong. This is my property and I'll ask you to please leave it." Our lawyer in Milford called me and begged that I explain to Snow that he could not keep the sheriff from carrying out his lawful business. It seemed the woman in question had put up fifty dollars to have a hearing on the gun. Frank carefully removed a small device in the gun and let it be held in the sheriff's office pending the outcome of the case. The lady lost it; the gun was returned, but the whole affair upset Frank and Snow because of the stupidity and injustice of it all. We paid for the lawyer and were the first to learn the outcome. This again was a case in which the earlier employers had been having domestic altercations!

Snow

Frank hayed all the cows and fed the calves. He also took a basket of hay out to the sheep, which by now numbered six, due to lambing. He made a path out there even through the snow in winter. He was devoted to all animals. We hoped he would stay on alone, as he had done most of the cooking and housework before, but he was too lonely and left to stay with a married son and two fine grandsons.

One very fine thing grew out of this relationship. Snow's obsession about men seemed to ease up. Frank was elderly and a true friend. The calls from his son didn't upset our routine, and no ugly thoughts disturbed Snow. The smoggy air was definitely clearing.

About a year after our settlement in Ponemah, my father was faced with a decision. In the fall he drove down from Temple and wanted to know if he could find some way to move nearer to us after their return from the Cambridge apartment. Snow and I conferred about this for some time. My mother was becoming a self-induced invalid and would need special household help even though Father was retired. They had always been in comfortable means, but Mother's gifted, temperamental personality had to be handled by close family members. In their eighties they must have realized this, although Mother never really tried to adjust. By this time, she did allow Father to make plans without thwarting him.

There were a number of unspoken questions in my mind. Snow and I needed no complicating interference. We had tried to give up living on the philosophy of what "they" might think. We dressed for comfort and worked at what we wanted when we wanted. No one was planning our lives but ourselves. I spent sometime with an earlier friend, a psychiatrist. Having a brother and a sister, who seemed in much better positions to undertake our parents' last years than I, it might almost be unfair to joggle the new foundations I was in the process of putting down. My first marriage was directly tied to mistakes they had made in preventive measures, a sort of on-again, off-again attitude. This was twenty-six years earlier, but ten of those years had been a period of depression not shared by them in love or help. My doctor suggested that it was the greatest compliment my father could give in choosing me to support him in this last need of his. He was proving that he had always trusted and loved me, but his hands had been tied, in some manner, all the past years. This was a profound observation. My mother had used me at her whim but was

Mr. Somebody

so jealous that she couldn't leave us together if she heard us laughing or exchanging good stories. In her late years she liked to eat off a tray in the sitting room or upstairs while Father and his guests ate in the dining room. She had a lot of suffering to do. After I caught on to this, I avoided what might be construed as subtle, private jokes with Father, although he was an honest, dedicated, devoted, joke-spinning man. He could still have worn his wedding suit with his heart on its sleeve.

Snow was in awe of Mother. She was formidable. Her moods changed like New England weather, only faster. But he spoke only when spoken to and used so much tact he had avoided any controversial subject. In fact, he had never ruffled her feathers, ever. One affirmative vote. Father would expect me to plan a house, place it where I wished, and oversee its building. Two affirmative votes. The house would be large enough for an attendant and a housemaid. My idea was to plan it for my daughter, still childless, when she and her husband returned, this time from his Korean tour of duty. He had been in the service for three years during World War II, in the European theater, and, this time they were being sent from post to post in the United States. I knew this plan might be fun while designing the house, but I doubted that the young people would ever really use it, since the husband, Bob, was very difficult to satisfy. One negative vote. Snow had been the only one to get along with Bob while in Sudbury, because he agreed on all matters and played it dumb most of the time. Bob had felt unchallenged.

My siblings refused to have their parents live near or with them. At the same time they plainly showed their jealousy of my having been selected to care for them. This was an extremely negative objection, which indeed caused many years of tense conditions, ending in a complete breakdown in relations ten long years later.

A very strong and private reason came through *me* for Snow—not *for* me. Father and Snow had a fine time together. Father lived in chinos and sneakers and loved the informal life of country and farm living. His city-person was a complete and different entity. If we drove father to a Harvard Club reunion or a board meeting, we left him at a point where my brother or an associate could pick him up. It didn't bother us, because we really didn't want any Boston clothing or streets! It's possible Snow never saw far into his in-laws' background, or he might have felt out of place. But the comfortable honor bestowed on Snow was the last necessary step in releasing him from his strangling past memories. The scales were tipped by the affirmative votes. It took most of the winter, sending plans back and forth between

Denver and Amherst, before my daughter and I worked out a suitable, functional Cape Cod reproduction home. Ground was broken and the foundation poured before the frost was entirely out of the site. It accomplished its first mission that summer: an absorbing interest for my parents. They came down each Thursday for the afternoon and tea. We kept a photograph album of its progress.

Snow and I put enough granite foundation rocks, uncovered near the original barn, on the stone boat and hauled them over so that the main house would sit on old-time gray granite. Even though our sprawling house and sheds were all Venetian red, my mother would not accept our creed, "Any color, as long as it's red!" She settled for gray with old-red trim. The house was planned with their early family furniture in mind; windows spaced, doors swung, two fireplaces on the ground floor, with bedroom and bath in an ell suite. The upstairs was arranged so that it could be used as a separate apartment if that were needed.

Once in a while social or business circumstances forced us to divide up. Father might stop and ask Snow to do an errand with him even while we were waiting for a salesman or repairman. Snow always went, but I could tell that he was suffering deep inside. He'd hesitate before answering, to allow his mind to cover the opportunities he left behind him. No one else noticed. If he could not be overheard, he'd tell me to be good. In other circumstances he might not look at me at all. During his absence I would actually do enough new things or make certain changes, such as cut out a sleeveless blouse or take down the china and dust all the shelves. As soon as we could be alone after his return, he would demand a review of what I had done. Just to tell him I had read a few chapters, watched television, or straightened up the living room would never wipe out his doubts. Something tangible—a completed physical two-hour job —could wipe out his fear before it could be formed. It could be excised from his thoughts. But if I had stayed outside to weed the flowerbeds or cut a piece of lawn, I could achieve nothing to help him. He had to accept me as innocent by reason of an indoor, time-consuming activity. Over the years the conscious necessity skipped by me, and I stood naked with a stammered, though truthful recitation. Then two days of horror would have to pass.

We became guardians of a young boy who attended the local school. He stayed with us for five years, and we did see that he was educated and learned good manners. He turned into an attractive man, married an intelligent girl, and now has three children and his

Mr. Somebody

Snow driving the hay chopping rig in 1952 with Father's house in left background.

own business. When Arthur turned fourteen I realized my error in judgment. Snow saw him as a competitor or as someone who might grow closer to me than him. Here I was raising a young man as a third member in our household whom Snow suddenly classified as a threat; the situation did bring back many of his worst symptoms. I stuck it out because we had a couple living near the barn and my parents next door, and, with so many added ways to juggle the numbers game, I was sure I could turn every new threat toward Snow's favor. He would have to become inured to all such situations and trust me in the midst of any confusion, or there would be no complete cure of his neurosis. It was manipulating the environment, all right—but it appeared to be the logical moment to step into danger. Our exclusion of the world had lasted at least five years but, under these changing circumstances, we had to attempt a normal succession of life's events.

Then up popped an unprecedented request. My parents would

make a visit with their son in Concord, Massachusetts, while Snow and I arranged with a mover, selected what furniture would be chosen from a larger house, set everything in place, and when every rug and dish was in place, they'd return to the completed Pasture House. We sent down those things that had been in the family six generations and all their favorite pictures and bric-a-brac. We worked all day. After the second day, we worked all night, putting in place clocks, mirrors, scarves, and even ashtrays. The dishes and silver were on shelves and in drawers, food in the refrigerator and cupboards; trays and linens in obvious places. The beds were made up; Father's tobacco jar and pipes were on a large table by his favorite chair. Lamps, tall and short, were in place with shades to match the selected rugs. The dining room had a morning-sunny bay window for breakfasting. Mantels held their favorite ornaments, including a wonderful carved monkey, high on a stump, with spectacles on, reading a morning paper. Mother's bedside table held everything she ever used, and her electric pad was plugged in near her bed, ready for use. Even their clothes were hung in two closets. When we left early that morning the house looked lived in already.

Father strolled over after he had tucked Mother into her bed with a book; he was astounded! They never moved an item and never had to hunt around for anything. Everything was within view or at hand. Andirons and screens were at their places and fires were laid ready to strike a match found in brass holders tacked up near the mantels. What a willing man my Snowie proved to be! He had milked his cows as usual and snatched cups of coffee on the run. Later, we emptied the Temple house by dividing the remaining items between the three children. Snow and I had to empty the attic and move three thousand books the others did not want. The space under the hot roof was crowded by a collection of trunks and papers covering many generations. It did, of course, fall on us to do what others should have faced many years before! The other siblings chose and left.

We trimmed a path between the sheep pen and the manmade sky-pond below it. We fitted a gate so the cows couldn't slip onto the lawn of Pasture House. Our fence had to be moved because the house site actually was originally in the sheep pasture. Father traveled that path twice a day to pick up his car. This was our plan to keep in close touch with him. Once a day I used it for my teatime calls.

Mr. Somebody

Mother never left that home. She must have set her mind on that. She neither came over to our house nor went out for another automobile drive with us or Father. The practical nurse, who came at my asking, ran the household. Their housekeeper drove down from Temple to keep the house clean and do extra cooking. Father drove out twice a day on errands: first it was five miles to the post office, then a round robin of stops for hardware and his home food supplies. I had arranged for a local doctor, interested in geriatrics, to make a weekly call at the house. Mother would not eat, though there was nothing wrong with her. But the call always gave Father a lift, and he was pleased if there was something he could get or do for Mother. He'd loved mother with total devotion, since he was sixteen years old.

Mother lingered only through the winter. That was her intention. She had been beautiful and gifted, but she had nothing left except a keen mind, which she kept buried in books. She read a book a day, had read all the classics in poetry, theater, and prose. Since then she read books on international subjects and by controversial and modern writers—everything. She could recall and discuss anything, especially interracial improvement or international compatibility. She was withdrawn from her social environment because she had lost her leadership.

We had a call late one night for medicine. Mother had had a sudden attack of pneumonia. We telephoned the druggist, and Snow and I drove over to meet him at his store—after we had all three dressed! Mother responded but was later moved to a nursing home accompanied by her own nurse. My broken father had seen me alone and said simply, "I cannot sleep with Jane any longer." I spoke to the doctor and told him quite simply that things had changed at Pasture House. It was he who had made the arrangements. Two weeks later it was over.

Father and Snow became very close. Mother's name was never mentioned by anyone. While Father spent a night with his son, I had to remove *everything* in the house that might remind him of his adored wife. He could not hold up otherwise. Since Snow knew little of Father's background, he didn't even look for subjects to avoid. They chatted happily about boyhood pranks, fishing, jokes, and stories. A miracle took place for both of them.

For about five years we kept Pasture House going as usual. The housekeeper spent half a week there cleaning and cooking enough for

Snow

holidays and weekends. Each summer Father dedicated himself to the haying. He had his important part to play in turning switches to "off" and "on" for the unloader, and in hustling over to the grain store if we ran out of baling twine. He fitted his plans around our need for him. This was part of the plan, of course. We believed that any man who had spent his life at the helm should feel needed and believe he was the captain of his ship, even if that ship was reduced to a rowboat or a punt with a pole. He had worked with success all his life and, as I read the future, such a man should never feel unwanted or superfluous. He should be the master of his life, answer his own front door, and keep his checkbook under his own signature.

There was no service for Mother. All concerned felt it would be safer to give Father a little time to gather himself into his earlier public image. When the wildflowers were in bloom again, other family members and friends gathered in Weston for a commemoration. Snow drove Father, as he now called him, to Concord so that my brother could take him the rest of the way.

During 1954 we were overtaken by the thought that Snow's natural father might still be alive. We made considerable efforts to locate him. We three had been driving to Maine at least twice a year, even spending a night now and then. Father enjoyed such trips if we went informally, ate at roadside stands, and stayed in cabins. I had worked out a list of nonperishable foods to take in a basket so that, with a Sterno stove, we could have breakfast coffee or tea with powdered cream and rolls to go with fruit juices. It worked into a highly successful touch of housekeeping. With a complete unit, we could take enough for all types of meals without having to rely on food that needed refrigeration. Father turned in early, so Snow and I curled up together to watch television.

We were still making our trips in the cab of a small pickup truck with me in the middle. I did drive after dark—but generally I was sitting stiff and unstirring in a backbreaking position. My legs shared the space with the gearshift and raised metal box cover; my vision ahead was contracted by the space left around the rear-view mirror and a windshield divider.

We made a few inquiries around the Brunswick area, but although we found a reference to an elderly Horace McKenney, we never located anyone by that name. A letter from Parker B. Stinson, registrar at the division of vital statistics in Augusta, Maine, made us shrink

Mr. Somebody

Father during the late 1950s.

Snow

from the idea of locating the family. Perhaps the contact would bring more misfortune than fortune, in the nonmercenary sense.

After these forages we switched to tracking down some of Father's earlier forebears. His grandfather started his pastorate in Eastport, Maine. It seemed impossible to believe now, but we actually drove all the way to that most easterly point in the United States of America. We found a room in a then-abandoned government building that had been sold to a family for use as a roominghouse. This was part of President Roosevelt's glamorous idea of harnessing the tides at Passamaquoddy Bay.

We spent a day hunting up churches but located only one young minister, and he was busy with a picnic-headed group of youngsters. We didn't find the houses and streets mentioned in the family diaries, but we noted the worn-out wharves, the empty sardine factories, and the distressed waterfront areas. While standing on one wharf, where rail tracks entered, we watched a ferry, crossing from Lubec, piled high with Puss-in-Boots catfood already in its neat cans. All three of us felt the dreary end of an active, successful outpost of American fishing industry. Eastport was a large town running up hills and out onto spits of land, ending now with broken-down pilings, the poles missing or leaning with the weight of rotting platforms. They looked like giant spiders or the shadow of a daddy longlegs.

The tide was out, so Snow and I could climb down a narrow path to the water level. There we found a rotting rowboat with a frayed painter or cordage still holding its responsibility to a ring that rose and lowered with the tides. The shanty held an ancient beach wagon, some tackle, a lobster-pot weight, broken buoys: man's work shown by hands now departed. This was a touching spot. Glory had been this easterly spearhead; but disuse and regression, the departure of the simple enough sardine, had broken the spear. We rejoined Father at the top but could only look out across the muddy-bottomed cover of the past great port that had been Eastport.

After ten years of marriage my daughter had three living children quite close together. Sewing, knitting, and crotcheting baby clothes and creating winter outfits were happy occupations for me. More and more often I begged off from the afternoon local trips, and as a result Snow and Father spent more time together. Work piled up for Snowie; the farm chores began to suffer, and he began to lose weight and look tired. He was attempting far too much. Being a dairyman takes long

Mr. Somebody

hours, physical labor, thought, and rest periods. Getting up early to rush through work and then making a day's trip somewhere that brought him home late for the milking was overtaxing his limits. After the last cow and calf were attended, he was shaky. Too many cups of coffee were dosing him with too much caffein. During the nights I could count 140 beats per minute of his overworked heart. He changed to 97 percent caffein-free for his coffee breaks, and this helped a great deal. Only once had he consented to have a physical checkup, and that one caused such sweating and quaking that the doctor diagnosed a serious nervous condition and prescribed tranquilizers! Snowie will not even touch aspirin; a nap removes his headaches. His system works so perfectly that he has never touched cough medicine. So far, he has never been ill, and he can toss off a cold in two days! He makes the point to me that he never wants to know what might be wrong. "I'll wait and see what happens. Time enough then when I'll have to." Having his Grammy die in his arms without warning and still believing she had seen no doctor had given him an immovable resolution.

Father was alone in his house at night, four hundred feet across the fields. I found I was watching for his lights, the rooms they emanated from, and the times they showed. I could follow his movements through his evenings and during his nights. I began to worry and lose sleep. Every day he was at his door if we drove by; he needed a constant sharer. All the time he did not spend doing odd jobs or automobile errands he spent on a bench under our heavy maple tree. At times we'd find him on the makeshift bench by our pond, watching the ducks, tears always in his eyes.

Snow and I were safe. He had found an idol whom he called Father and for whom he found extraordinarily appropriate sentiments for Christmas and Father's Day. They had worked out a routine that was running like a fine clock. But I saw a physician to ask whether we could be wearing ourselves out with so little time for our own marriage. A solution came to us one night: add a few rooms on to our house; lend our living room with its fireplace; break a door through to a kitchenette, den, bath and bedroom. Father jumped at the idea. Plans were again drawn out, and a carpenter went right to work. The newest ell blended in well with our spreading red home. We hung a very old front door, and he put on an antique knocker. Father had his own front door as well as his mahogany, silver, and crystal sherry carafe and stemmed glasses in his dining area. He sat on a seat outside his entrance on the terrace outlined with lilacs.

Snow

We advertised an auction and sold 48 registered Jerseys and all our haymaking equipment. We kept some young heifers and 2 riding horses. There would have been no meaning in life for Snowie without dogs, cats, pigeons, bantams, ducks, turkeys, sheep, and geese; and some indoor birds and hamsters for me and the grandchildren. At our height we had to be sure that 110 mouths were fed before we slept at night! So, in disposing of the cows, I had to keep his interest in life important to him. His contribution toward his livelihood was work, not wages. It took a great deal of reassurance from Father and myself to make Snow accept the fact that he was carrying a man's remunerative position.

The sharp shrinkage in numbers meant he had time to give to Father. The latter was in his chosen place at six o'clock for the evening television news; Snow touched off the fire, and I brought them two trays at six-thirty every night. By nine, Father rose and went to bed. Snow would rejoin me after I had the dishes put away. We locked ourselves together in our private ell and watched a movie and the late news.

For a time I thought I had sacrificed Snow for my father's sake, but it worked in reverse. This had been my original hope, but I had not realized that we would have to break up the use of our beautiful barn and lose our fancy Jerseys. It brought my emancipation. Snow now called me Mother, and life was calm between us. Trust had grown as strong as Mount Monadnock.

Snow and I didn't look our age, but neither did Father. We passed for the same age. The answer must have lain in the fact that I took the initiative in all decisions in what must have appeared as a rather imperious manner.

In one week, ten years after Mother had died, Father was driving his car and twice knicked another by misjudging the width of a parking space in the Milford Oval. It was a warning, of course, and Snow and I plotted to keep Father off the road as much as possible without his noticing the change. Snowie took Father for the mail trip each morning, and we took him out every good day for some trip after the two men had had their after-luncheon naps. On a Monday he went down to see his surgeon; by Wednesday he was brought back by his son. He stumbled through the door saying, "I'm done for." We drove him to the Phillips House on Friday. He was in the hospital for two weeks, but even though he was my father and lived with us, the nurses and doctors would tell me nothing of his condition. When Daddy first saw me he asked, "Is it cancer?"

Mr. Somebody

"Why," I said, "don't you know? They've tried to pin that on you for years and never succeeded." That was all that was said. He seemed satisfied and worked himself back onto his feet. When he left the hospital, he went to Concord for a few days while I prepared for his final homecoming. I had learned that he might live six months but not more than eight.

We rejoiced at his return and went on as before. We fed him excellent food, kept him busy watching baseball games, and driving anywhere and everywhere with him. He even drove his car again, and after six months all the earlier looks and strength reappeared. It was a miracle, but we kept his spirits at a high peak and tossed aside his reference to "It's over."

We could never find a nurse or attendant, except for seven inter- mittent nights, after we had kept him active for fourteen months. It was all Snow's doing. What a perfect relationship! Snow never failed to be with Father at six every evening, even his last one. It was during "Gunsmoke," which they both enjoyed. The fire crackled on the hearth, and the nurse had returned at seven, after a weekend off. He had rallied following his first bad morning, and I had taken them soup and cake for supper on their trays. I slipped over to Pasture House to see our tenants, an unworried family, for a few minutes. I had a call almost at once: "Better come home." It had been quite simple. Father had fallen into Snow's lap, and the nurse and he had laid him on the bed. His other children had not driven up to see him. This last moment was covered by a short exchange by telephone with his son. "There is nothing I can do tonight," he informed Snow. "I'll be there in the morning." He picked up the details after our part was com- pleted.

Snow and I were not consulted further. Our family had been among those who had brought Unitarianism to America, but my sister, the eldest child, ran every further plan from Massachusetts. She had become a social Episcopalian, and I learned from a cousin the service in Weston was heavily High Church and the Unitarian minis- ter was not one that had close ties to the family. The fieldstone church was so full there were not enough seats for everyone. Even at eighty- seven, having retired at sixty-five and living away from Weston for twenty-two years, his friends and relatives were many and devoted. He had been the nearly perfect man and friend.

Snow

No one thanked Snow, but he and I were jointly elated that we had cared for the living, even while so many others cared for the dead. That is our philosophy.

Essentially, quite understandably, Snow was a shy and, unconsciously, a cautious man. Even though for many years he was manageable, pliable, and seemingly a yes man, he remained at the same time very doubtful about the motives of mankind. He had had to trust his grandmother Meader when he was in his home in Brunswick or her home in Boothbay Harbor. He felt an uncanny distrust of his uncles, Snow and Frank, but couldn't take a stand against them when he was fourteen. They used their wives as cajolers, for even they felt the animosity of Snowden toward themselves. But he acquiesced to the plans and trusted their words. I cannot imagine how a sunny, outgoing, handy boy could be so suddenly turned into a solemn, introverted lad. It was perhaps the traumatic realization that they all had tricked him with lies, much as Ananias and Sapphira had done, that caused this change in his personality. He certainly did the heavy work on Fiske Avenue without resistance while his sister played tweeny to their girl cousins. As punishment for himself, Uncle Snow accused the orphans of stealing and lying, released his aggressions by whipping his nephew with the leather strap. But it was the dichotomy within the character of this uncle that drove our Snowie out on his own at sixteen years.

He had hoped to be as tall as his family; he made up for this lack of satisfaction by a show of strength rather than by pugnaciousness. Snow has no recollection of scuffles. Even the man who boxed his ears didn't get a kick on the shins or a bite on the hand. "I was a little shaver," he tells me, "and ran like a son of a gun." He played big brother to a much smaller and younger sister. Grammy drummed on that thesis. He'd stick up for her, if not for himself, during their early childhood.

Sawing wood and beating rugs kept him from his chances to play ball and make friends in Waltham. He had liked baseball in Maine and was popular with all the children on his hill who attended the district school. His last present had been a bicycle, which he was allowed to take to Massachusetts. Anytime he was free he explored the local

Mr. Somebody

streets on that bike. It spelled freedom. He still had no friends of his age. They had left all his clothes, toys, cart, and special treasures behind on Bay Street and rebuilt his life with entirely unfamiliar outfits. He sold that bicycle when he left Fiske Avenue.

A terrifying shyness overtook him. Even now he looks down at his feet when meeting people, and he has to be forced into making inquiries from strangers. Father and I used to laugh if Snowie went into a village store to locate an address in an unfamiliar town. If I couldn't overhear the directions, it was worse than if those directions had never been given. "You go out there and follow the same way you're headin' now. About a mile down you'll hit a fork; there you take the left, and further along the second right. At the top of the next hill you'll find a dirt road. You can't miss them because the yard is full of chickens." Snow could never even remember whether we were to take the left or right at that first fork! He always lost on any fifty-fifty chance. He would have made a worthless accident witness.

For those who did learn to know him, it was a rare experience. Although he called me Miss June until he changed it to Mother, everyone called him Snow on first sight. He was never "Mr. Anybody." My grandchildren thought his name was Snowiedear, because I used it so much. With his handsome, interesting face, his full head of hair, his unassuming manner, and his casual clothes, some saw him as artist or poet. To hear his Down-East voice and inflection was to place him as a man of the north country.

One should try to love such people who lay a quiet foundation for others. The world nearly broke him, but he would have lain down his life for others to fall back upon. Tumult is on the surface today. The ocean bottom is a quiet, still place. He couldn't hurt an animal, even tattoo a calf's ear, but could drive two tons of Percherons. He could laugh and tease with the pairs of children who came up each summer from Harlem as "Fresh Air Camp" selections, or take his dog on a solitary twilight walk.

He told someone the other day, "I can be happy anywhere." This shows his massive faith in this world and his wife. His circle is small, but within it his hands are always busy and his days lived one at a time. He is a "Mr. Somebody" in his unworldly and inconspicuous way.

Snow

Postscriptum

A SEQUEL, OUTCOME, some reassurance, or added facts—are these what would satisfy you? Can a mentally disturbed man be permanently cured?

There is one noticeable residual trait observed as such by the author. It passes as slight deafness, or inattention, or perhaps a certain social ineptness. When young people are present, being asked what they'd like to do or have or eat, Snow breaks in with, "Am I supposed to wait? Don't I get a choice? I live here, don't I? How come the kids come first these days?" Generally, he had misread the plans. This may be only a snack offered the children, with dinner being served later. His treat may already be at his place. It is a quick, automatic response that he cannot control even though he recovers very quickly. Snow and I spent some time on these seeming dissents with the children. Our conclusions have become one. He had so little childhood after leaving "home" in Maine that he is sure no child appreciates today what he feels he missed yesterday. He knows he would do better with the present-day opportunities if he had what today's children are being offered for their tomorrows.

Snow is so generous with his time and energy that he would sacrifice both to anyone who asked a favor. He would not hurt man or creature if he knew how to avoid doing so.

He drives a car slowly and obeys all rules of etiquette on the road: dims his lights for the passing rear driver's safety and eye comfort; allows a car to find an opening in a line; pulls up to lights as they turn yellow. If he finds himself leading a parade, he puts on his right-turn signal and pulls up to let them all go ahead to resume their choice of pace.

Snow takes no part in the wider world around him, but he works long hours at home to make the money and time count. He rises an hour earlier than the household to read *Newsweek, Yankee Magazine,* a daily, or any article I put out for his attention. When tired he naps. But for his hazel eyes, he now looks like the Stuart portrait of President Washington. His gray-white hair is still full-headed and combed back to hide those curls. He is handsome and trim. He is a quieted man. He is a happy man. His relationships are normal.

J.G. / 1980

If I can stop one heart from breaking,
I shall not live in vain;
If I can ease one life the aching,
Or cool one pain,
Or help one fainting robin
Unto his nest again,
I shall not live in vain.

Emily Dickinson

List of Illustrations

Place of Birth *Topsham, Maine*

Street .... No. ....

Child's Name *Snow McKenn*

Date of Birth *April 16, 1903*

Sex *M* Color *W*

Living or Stillborn ....

No. of Child, 1st, 2nd, etc. *1st*

No. of children of this mother now living ....

Father's Name *Horace C. McKen*

" Color or Race *W* Age

" Birthplace *Lisbon Falls, Ma*

" Residence *Topsham, Ma*

Street .... No. ....

Father's Occupation *Mill Worker*

Mother's Maiden Name *Cora Clara Mea*

" Color or Race *W* Age

" Residence *Topsham, Ma*

" Birthplace *Boothbay Harbor*

" Occupation *Housewife*